Plant-Based on a Budget QUICK & EASY

ALSO AVAILABLE FROM TONI OKAMOTO

Plant-Based on a Budget
The Friendly Vegan Cookbook

The Plant-Powered People Podcast | PlantPoweredPodcast.com
More Budget Recipes | PlantBasedonaBudget.com
Vegan Food & Lifestyle Website | FoodSharingVegan.com
Plant-Based Meal Plans | PlantBasedMealPlan.com

CONNECT WITH TONI:

@plantbasedonabudget
@plantbasedonabudget
Facebook.com/PlantBasedonaBudget

Plant-Based on a Budget QUICK & EASY

100 Fast, Healthy, Meal-Prep, Freezer-Friendly, and One-Pot Vegan Recipes

Toni Okamoto

BenBella Books, Inc.
Dallas, TX

Food photographs by Alfonso Revilla Photography
Lifestyle photographs by Lauren Alisse Photography

BenBella Books, Inc.
10440 N. Central Expressway
Suite 800
Dallas, TX 75231
benbellabooks.com
Send feedback to feedback@benbellabooks.com

BenBella is a federally registered trademark.

Printed in the United States of America
10 9 8 7 6 5 4 3 2

Library of Congress Control Number: 2022021605
ISBN 9781637742495 (trade paperback)
ISBN 9781637742501 (ebook)

Editing by Claire Schulz and Aurelia d'Andrea
Copyediting by Karen Wise
Proofreading by Ashley Casteel
Indexing by Debra Bowman
Text design and composition by Aaron Edmiston
Cover design by Sarah Avinger
Printed by Versa Press

To my dad, with all my love, respect, and admiration.
All the nights and weekends you brought me along as you worked overtime are deeply ingrained in my heart, and I have so much gratitude for the sacrifices you made as a young, single father to give me the best life. Thank you for showing me what hard work looks like. This book, and everything I do, is in your honor.

CONTENTS

One-Pot Meals

30-Minute Meals

Sheet Pan Dishes and Casseroles

Mix-and-Match Bowls

Proteins

FOREWORD

Let's be real: Every one of us lives on a budget.

That budget is primarily a financial restriction for some, but, even for those who can afford to buy whatever food they'd like, living on a time budget is often a daily reality.

These days, who has time to balance the rigors of working, taking care of themselves and their dependents (human and nonhuman), *and* eating healthfully?

Too many of us have a seemingly never-ending list of to-dos begging for our time. This is a big reason why many of us spend less and less time preparing our own meals, relying instead on Uber Eats, meal kit deliveries, fast-food drive-thrus, and microwavable frozen dinners to quickly satiate our hunger each evening.

Not only are these options more expensive than preparing our own food, but such a shift away from home cooking has serious consequences for our health. After all, it's no longer a secret that much of the food served in restaurants or pre-packaged and prepared for pickup at the grocery store or delivered to our doorsteps is typically loaded with far too much oil, salt, and sugar, which keeps us coming back for more. Over time, this kind of diet may shrink our wallets while expanding our litany of health problems.

Is there a way we can enjoy delicious, nutritious plant-based food that's easy on our financial *and* time budgets? There is, and Toni Okamoto tells us how in *Plant-Based on a Budget Quick & Easy*.

Gone are the days when making your own meal required an hour of labor with questionable results at the end. Say goodbye, too, to the idea that only a trained chef can make something worth eating.

Toni shows us money- and time-saving tactics that allow us to enjoy delectable dishes while getting back precious time to do more of the things we want to do.

So, whether you're on a financial budget, a time budget, or both, sit back and prepare to be wowed by the tips and tricks Toni's about to teach you. I've been preparing plant-based meals for three decades, yet even I learned new things from reading this book. I'm confident you will, too, and that, because of Toni, you'll have more money and more time to enjoy both your food and the rest of your life.

MICHAEL GREGER, MD, FACLM
AUTHOR, *HOW NOT TO DIE*

INTRODUCTION

When I began my plant-based journey in 2007, my guiding stars were a heartfelt desire to help animals and a profound wish to live healthier. Back then, I hadn't yet learned to fully appreciate the value of time—that would come later—but I definitely knew the value of *money*. That's because, in short, I had none. When you're not on solid financial footing, thinking about how you're going to pay for things takes up *a lot* of brainspace.

In those lean early days, as I juggled two jobs and struggled to conquer my debt, I was fortunate to have the wherewithal to get really creative with meal planning and food shopping to make my newfound lifestyle work on a very tight budget.

When I went to the supermarket, I'd head right for the bulk bins, toting not just my own shopping bags but my own measuring cups, too, to make sure I wasn't wasting precious pennies on more ingredients than a recipe called for. (I'm sure this would embarrass some people, but it never bothered me.) I was determined to eat well and find a path to greater economic stability, and food costs weren't going to stand in my way!

It wasn't always easy, though—and it was definitely a learning process. I can still remember scraping my bowl at the end of a meal to ensure I didn't waste even a single grain of rice. It took me a while to learn the ropes, but eventually I got the hang of it, learning to maximize my spending to buy healthy basics so I could prepare meals that were both nourishing and affordable.

Looking back, I'm proud of my determination to find the most affordable plant-based meals; after all, they're what led me to launch my blog, *Plant-Based on a Budget*, and begin to inspire my loved ones to overcome a generational history of lifestyle-related illnesses and find *their* path toward healthy eating, too. Those ambitions also allowed me to transform my financial circumstances in ways I couldn't have imagined back when I was swimming in debt. It had never even occurred to me that I could build *Plant-Based on a Budget* into a thriving company, but when I got my first sponsorship offer—someone actually wanted to *pay* me to put their ad on my site!—I wondered what such an opportunity could lead to. To my great surprise, what began as a blog I'd write in between the hours I logged nannying, dog-walking, and house-sitting has since blossomed into four cookbooks, a podcast, and a full-time career. And the best part of it all is that I have found my true purpose in life helping people eat more plants, which in turn also helps create a kinder world for animals and the planet. I feel honored and grateful that through my work, I have been invited to help jumpstart so many plant-based journeys.

The success of *Plant-Based on a Budget* has completely transformed my economic circumstances, and I couldn't be more grateful for this twist of fate. And while I still avoid wasting food, I no longer obsess and get stressed about every penny spent and every grain of rice. Today, I've shifted my focus to saving *time*. This creates more space in my life for the things I really love, like hanging out with friends and family, helping animals, and dreaming up new ways to make the world a better place.

If you're like me and want to spend less time in the kitchen preparing food, cooking, and cleaning, and more time doing things that really light you up, this book is for you! Of course, helping you save money will still be my priority, but just as I spent years figuring out the best ways to cut back on food costs, I've also dedicated countless hours to figuring out all the smartest methods for saving time on food prep, which I'll share in a moment. Besides helping you create mouthwatering meals you and your family will love, this book will also help you get to the fun part—eating!—much faster and more easily. But first, a word to those who might be just embarking on their own plant-based journeys.

START WHERE YOU ARE

Some people embrace plant-based eating with the passion of a new convert, diving in headfirst and never looking back. This was not how my journey unfolded.

My approach was far more tentative (a longtime Taco Bell taco habit will do that to you!) and involved many starts and stops. My heart was in the right place, but I was living paycheck to paycheck and didn't always prioritize healthy eating, instead opting for whatever was readily available and, as often was the case, whatever was free.

Fast-forward 16 years, and eating plant-based is second nature for me. I don't even have to think about it—I just do it! But I know that most of the people who follow *Plant-Based on a Budget*, and perhaps you yourself, aren't at that place yet. And that's okay. My philosophy has always been "progress over perfection," and testing the waters is part of the process. But I'm willing to bet that if you follow the advice and recipes in this cookbook, you'll eventually find that plant-based eating brings you so many benefits that you'll come to a place where you don't want to look back. I know that was the case for me. So, celebrate your wins, and give yourself a break if and when you struggle. The next day (or the next meal!) is a brand-new opportunity.

What would have helped me immensely when I first set off on my plant-based journey was a guide like this to show me how easy and affordable it is to eat healthfully without meat, eggs, or dairy. (Or fast-food beef tacos!) And if you're like me and your free time is at a premium, being able to pull together delicious, nourishing meals quickly is a major priority. So I hope this book can be a truly useful resource you'll turn to again and again. Getting to help others on their journey gives me great joy, especially when it means saving you time to enjoy your life more.

TIME IS MONEY: HOW TO SET YOURSELF UP FOR SUCCESS

In my book *Plant-Based on a Budget*, I presented a step-by-step plan for spending as little money as possible on scrumptious, healthy food. In this book, you'll discover all the tools and strategies for eating well without a huge time investment. After all, time is money, and I want you to have plenty of both!

So let's talk about some of the ways I budget both time and money, in and out of the kitchen.

Meal Planning

Meal planning is where the money- and time-saving magic happens. From cutting down on your impulse purchases to minimizing your trips to fast-food drive-thrus, planning ahead has so many benefits—including creating more time for the things you really love and want to direct your attention to. And it will make your time in the kitchen preparing meals feel effortless. Really!

Meal planning can look different, depending on the person. Some people like creating detailed, color-coded spreadsheets that chart the course for breakfast, lunch, dinner, and snacks, and include all the nutrition information for a whole month of meals. Others simply pick a couple of recipes to batch-cook for the upcoming week's dinners. My personal style recently is to use my pressure cooker on a Sunday to batch-cook a protein like lentils or beans, plus a grain like rice or quinoa, and then turn to the Mix-and-Match Bowls chapter of this book during the workweek for vegetables and a homemade or store-bought sauce. It makes weeknights so much easier when you have half of your meal prepared! Whichever strategy you choose, I'm positive that you'll feel the benefits once you get started. If you'd like a ready-made meal plan to get you started, check out the back of this book, where you'll find a week-long plan (and shopping list) based on recipes in this book. (I also offer lots of freebies at PlantBasedonaBudget.com/cookbook, where you can find free ebooks, a downloadable planner, and more.)

A Well-Stocked Pantry

As you already know, I'm all about cutting corners in the kitchen to save time. Because I like to take shortcuts, I'm always stocked up on pre-chopped frozen produce, canned beans, vegetable bouillon paste, canned tomatoes and tomato sauce, jarred garlic, and other products that make life a little easier. (Note, for broth, I prefer Better Than Bouillon brand's "No Chicken" base and that's what I used in my recipe testing. But you can have success with other veggie broth if that is what you have.)

You'll see those convenient products mentioned throughout my recipes, but please feel free to use fresh, frozen, and canned items interchangeably. The other part of me (that's much more relaxed) is a gardener who grows a large portion of the produce we eat in the summer, so I understand those of you who like to eat as fresh as possible. This book has something for everyone.

Time-Saving Kitchen Tools

I stick by what I said in *Plant-Based on a Budget*: you don't need fancy equipment to get started. As you can see in the photo below, I meal-prepped an entire week's worth of food using food storage containers from Dollar Tree. (Although I no longer use disposable plastic bags, back then I was grateful for the option, since I couldn't afford reusable silicone bags.)

If you have a budget for investing in kitchen equipment, you can see my favorites at PlantBasedonaBudget.com/shop. The following list covers the essentials, as well as some bonus equipment you may want to invest in when your budget allows—kitchen tools can be pricey up front, but the right ones will end up saving you more time and money in the long run.

Airtight containers—Whether you're hopping on the meal prep trend or storing leftovers, airtight containers are your best friends for keeping food fresh. I prefer glass containers with snap-on lids because they're great for freezing and they're microwave safe, but my husband finds them too clunky in his lunchbox and prefers lightweight plastic containers. There are also great insulated stainless steel containers for keeping soups warm (ideal if you don't have access to a microwave or kitchen at work).

Mason jars—These can be found at many supermarkets and are great for storing your bulk ingredients and prepared items like overnight oats, dressings, leftover soups and stews—you name it. They come in many sizes, and you may want a variety depending on what you'll use them for. I find a solid lunch- or dinner-sized helping of a meal will fit well in a 16-ounce jar. You can also buy used jars at thrift stores and purchase new lids online if they're rusty.

Reusable silicone bags—Because I try to avoid single-use plastic, reusable

silicone bags have become staples in our home. They're an up-front investment, but if you use them as often as we do for snacks, freezing, and marinating, you'll wind up saving more money than you would purchasing plastic bags. I recommend buying them in a variety of sizes.

Half sheet pans (aka rimmed baking sheets); 9 x 13-inch and 9 x 9-inch baking dishes—You'll need these for all the yummy recipes in the Sheet Pan Dishes and Casseroles chapter.

Loaf pan and muffin tin—These baking pans are generally very inexpensive and easy to find at thrift stores. You'll need them to create my easy quick breads and muffins (as well as the delicious cupcakes in the desserts chapter).

Large pot and skillet—To make soups, stews, and one-pot meals, grab a large saucepan or soup pot. You'll also want a large skillet for sautéing veggies, cooking up pancakes, and more.

Silicone baking mat—This has been a huge saver of time and money in my kitchen. Instead of using parchment paper on my sheet pan to make cookies and other baked treats, I throw this down. It saves me from scrubbing down the pan every time I use it, and from having to shell out cash each time I run out of parchment paper—and there's nothing to throw in the trash.

Blender, immersion blender, or food processor—There are quite a few recipes in this book that call for a blender or food processor. In general, blenders are suited for blending solid and liquid ingredients together. An immersion blender does the same, but rather than pouring your ingredients into a pitcher on a stand, you immerse the blender right into the cup/bowl/pot you're using to cook. Meanwhile, food processors prepare all sorts of foods in different ways (from chopping, shredding, and grinding ingredients to mixing up a dough) in much less time than doing those things by hand. So if I had to pick just one, it would probably be a food processor. I didn't have one until I received one as a wedding gift, and now I can't remember how I ever lived without it. Mine has an 8-quart capacity and came with slicing and shredding attachments. It's perfect! It slices and grates veggies literally in seconds.

Multifunction pressure cooker (such as Instant Pot)—Okay, so this is a splurge item, and you don't need one—you absolutely can make all the recipes in this book without it. But I'm including it because it revolutionized my meal preparation. This gadget cooks things in minutes, whereas making them on the stovetop or in a slow cooker could take hours. Better yet, once all the ingredients go into the cooker, no sautéing or stirring or flipping is required—allowing me to take a walk with my dog while dinner cooks. How cool is that?! Many of the recipes in this book have pressure cooker options, and it's also a great resource for making meals on road trips. You can cook just about anything in it, anywhere you can find an electric outlet!

Air fryer—Another splurge. This is the newest appliance in my kitchen, and I'm really loving how it allows me to use less oil. It's also more energy-efficient than firing up the oven and has the added benefit of not heating up my house during our hot Sacramento summers.

Smart Storage

Whenever I throw food in the compost bin because it's gone bad, it feels like throwing my hard-earned cash in the trash. It's tough on my heart, but 100 percent effective in reminding me that food waste is money waste.

One of the best tricks for avoiding food waste is proper storage to keep things fresh for as long as possible. You'll find directions for freezing in the freezer-friendly recipes in this book, but be sure to try these additional helpful tips to help your food last longer.

Parsley, cilantro, and other herbs—Using scissors or a sharp knife, snip the bottom off the herb stems and place them in a glass or jar of water as you would fresh-cut flowers. If you want them to last even longer, store the glass or jar in the refrigerator with a silicone or plastic bag loosely placed over it. If you're curious about a specific herb you have on hand, do a quick Google search for the best storage tips.

Leafy greens—I store kale and other sturdy greens the same way I store herbs: in a glass or jar of water in the refrigerator, like a bouquet of flowers. For more tender greens like spinach and lettuce, I store them in a resealable container along with a paper towel to help absorb any moisture and prevent them from becoming soggy.

Avocados—There's nothing worse than an avocado that has expired. To avoid this tragedy, I keep my underripe avocados on the counter and monitor them closely until they allow the slightest give in the squeeze test. As soon as that happens, I pop them in the refrigerator, which helps them last several extra days.

Carrots, celery, and citrus—Thoroughly wash your whole carrots, celery, lemons, and limes and place them in a large-mouth mason jar or other container, pour in enough water to cover, and put on the lid. You can store them in the refrigerator like this for up to 1 month.

Tofu—For savory dishes, I almost always use extra- or super-firm tofu that comes in vacuum-sealed packages. If I'm using only half the package, I store the leftover tofu in an airtight container filled with fresh water, making sure that the tofu is completely submerged. This way, it will stay fresh in the refrigerator for up to 5 days.

Freezer items—When freezing food for future meals, make sure you note the freeze date. One simple method I use is to take a piece of masking tape and use a Sharpie to write the name of the dish and the date it went into the freezer. I also have a magnetic whiteboard on my freezer that helps me keep track of what needs to be eaten and when.

When you're freezing soups and stews, remember to fill your containers no more than three-quarters of the way, in order to leave room for the liquid to expand as it freezes.

THE BASICS OF (QUICKER, EASIER) COOKING

Each of the recipes in this book is created to save you time in the kitchen, but I will say up front that some of them may look like they take a bit longer to prepare. Often that's because of a longer bake time (like some of the casserole recipes) or because a particular ingredient needs a longer inactive prep (like soaking overnight oats in the fridge or freezing tofu ahead of cooking to make it firmer). As much as possible, I kept the active prep time as short as possible—and the steps themselves as simple as can be—to make your life easy.

So, while you may need to plan ahead for some dishes, you won't need to spend hours chopping, stirring, and watching a pot! And many recipes are designed to make multiple servings so you can cook once and have enough to last you several meals. That way you can take full advantage of those opportunities when you have a little more time to spend in the kitchen, and then quickly reheat a meal on the following days when you're really pressed for time.

That said, it's totally possible to cook many recipes from this book and never spend more than 30 minutes on prep and cooking time combined! And if you're short on time, I recommend using pre-chopped vegetables, and never peeling your carrots or potatoes. I have a whole chapter devoted to dishes that come together in less than half an hour.

MY TOP TAKEAWAYS FROM THIS BOOK

Plant-Based Meal Planning Is Fun

When you think of meal planning, do you think "exciting"? You should! My trick to avoiding boring repetition and really relishing your food is by starting simple and adding new textures and flavors with each meal.

Let's take the Veggie-Packed Potato Leek Soup on page 58, for example. If I were making a big pot just for myself to eat throughout the week, I'd start by skipping the step to purée and would simply eat the vegetables whole on that first day. On the second day, I'd purée the soup for a different textural experience. On the third day, I'd pour some soup in my bowl, then add some hot sauce, crunchy croutons, and more black pepper. On the fourth day, I'd add sautéed greens and a squeeze of lemon juice. Switching up the tastes and textures really helps avoid meal burnout!

By the end of this book, you'll learn exactly how to extend the life of not only your big-batch meals but also your produce and batch-cooked weekly staples. Mastering proper storage and freezing techniques will go a long way. And the Mix-and-Match Bowls chapter will give you lots of options for sauces and additional ingredients you can serve on top of or alongside leftovers to make those leftovers feel new.

You Don't Need Meat

If you watch meal planning videos on YouTube and TikTok, you've noticed that there's definitely a formula for filling bento box–style containers. While some people add a piece of meat as their protein of choice, in the Mix-and-Match Bowls chapter of this book I will introduce you to some plant-based protein options. They're filling, nutritious, and—I promise—absolutely delicious.

Meal Prep Can Be Lightning Fast

There are so many ways to prepare meals, and it doesn't have to mean spending the day making lasagna or some other elaborate dish from scratch. It can be as simple as cooking a big pot of brown rice for the week, stocking up on a few cans of beans, some whole wheat tortillas, a jar of salsa, and an avocado. These ingredients can be mixed, matched, and transformed into a slew of tasty dishes in no time flat.

MAKE-AHEAD BREAKFASTS

Breakfast is rightly considered the most important meal of the day. But for many of us, finding time on busy mornings to prepare and enjoy this fundamental meal is practically mission impossible. Thankfully, I've unlocked the secret to a stress-free breakfast, and it's all in the prep work. Investing a little bit of time on the weekend to prep your meals for the week means having relaxed and delicious mornings, setting the tone for the entire day. It's truly a game-changer! All the recipes in this chapter can be made ahead or enjoyed right after you make them on those mornings when you do have time to take it slow.

FLUFFY FREEZER-FRIENDLY WAFFLES

Makes 4 to 6 full Belgian-style waffles | Ready in 30 minutes

Nothing kicks off the weekend better than a golden stack of homemade waffles. These are perfectly crisp on the outside, and light and fluffy on the inside—perfect for impressing brunch guests *and* for extending those Sunday Funday vibes to busy weekday mornings. You may want to make a double batch so you'll have a stash of waffles in the freezer for any time the mood strikes. See my tips for reheating these in just minutes.

Ingredients:

1 tablespoon flaxseed meal
2½ tablespoons warm water
1¾ cups vanilla plant-based milk
⅓ cup vegetable oil
1½ teaspoons vanilla extract
2 cups all-purpose flour
1½ tablespoons granulated sugar
1 tablespoon brown sugar
1 tablespoon baking powder
¼ teaspoon salt

Optional additions and swaps:

Swap the vanilla plant-based milk for plain
Swap the all-purpose flour for whole wheat flour or gluten-free flour
Add ½ teaspoon ground cinnamon in step 4
Stir in ½ cup blueberries or chocolate chips after step 4
Top with maple syrup
Top with vegan butter

Directions:

1. Turn on your waffle iron.
2. In a small bowl, whisk together the flaxseed meal and warm water for 1 minute. Set aside for 5 minutes to thicken.
3. In a large bowl, whisk together the plant-based milk, vegetable oil, vanilla, and flaxseed mixture.
4. Add the flour, both sugars, baking powder, and salt and whisk gently, just until combined. Make sure to not overmix.
5. Scoop the desired amount of batter onto the preheated waffle iron (you may need to experiment to find the amount that works best for yours). Follow your waffle iron instructions to cook. Repeat with the remaining batter until all the

waffles are cooked. Serve right away or freeze and reheat individual waffles as you like (see Toni's tips).

TONI'S TIPS:

>>Never mind store-bought frozen waffles—you can make these and freeze them for up to 3 months! Simply place the cooked waffles in a single layer on a baking sheet lined with a silicone mat or parchment paper and freeze for 2 hours, then store in a freezer bag or airtight container. To reheat, use a toaster (preferred), or loosely cover the waffles with aluminum foil and bake at 450 degrees for 3 to 5 minutes (depending on the size), or microwave in 45-second increments until warmed through.

MY TIPS:

ENDLESSLY CUSTOMIZABLE PANCAKES

Makes about 6 pancakes | Ready in 20 minutes

Consider this pancake recipe a blank slate to get creative with your favorite mix-ins—or try one of the 10 flavor options I suggest here! There's a little something to please any palate. And since they freeze well, you can have pancakes for breakfast any day of the week.

Ingredients:

1 tablespoon flaxseed meal
2½ tablespoons warm water
1¾ cups all-purpose flour
3½ tablespoons sugar
1 tablespoon baking powder
¼ teaspoon salt
1½ cups plant-based milk
3 tablespoons vegan butter, plus more for cooking
2 teaspoons vanilla extract

See the full recipe on page 28.

Flavor options:

Apple Cinnamon Pancakes: Add ⅓ cup finely diced apples + 1 teaspoon ground cinnamon in step 4

Banana Nut Pancakes: Add ½ cup mashed banana + ¼ cup chopped walnuts + 1 teaspoon ground cinnamon in step 4

Birthday Cake Pancakes: Add ⅓ cup rainbow sprinkles in step 4

Blueberry Lemon Pancakes: Add ⅔ cup blueberries + 1 tablespoon lemon juice + 1 tablespoon grated lemon zest in step 4

Carrot Cake Pancakes: Add ½ cup grated carrots + ¼ cup chopped walnuts + 1 teaspoon ground cinnamon in step 4

Double Chocolate Pancakes: Add 3 tablespoons cocoa powder + ½ cup vegan chocolate chips in step 4

Green Pancakes: Blend 2 cups spinach with the milk until completely smooth before adding in step 3

PB&S Pancakes: Melt ½ cup peanut butter and drizzle onto the cooked pancakes; serve with sliced strawberries

Pumpkin Spice Pancakes: Add 2 tablespoons puréed pumpkin + 1 teaspoon pumpkin pie spice (store-bought or page 216) in step 4

Zucchini Pancakes: Add ½ cup grated zucchini + 1 teaspoon ground cinnamon in step 4

Directions:

1. In a small bowl, whisk together the flaxseed meal and warm water for 1 minute. Set aside for 5 minutes to thicken.
2. In a large bowl, sift together the flour, sugar, baking powder, and salt.
3. Combine the plant-based milk and vegan butter in a medium microwave-safe bowl, and microwave until the butter is completely melted, about 1½ minutes.
4. Add the butter mixture, vanilla, and flaxseed mixture to the dry mixture and gently whisk just until the batter is smooth, but there's no need to remove all the lumps. Add your desired add-ins and flavorings. Do not overmix.
5. In a large nonstick skillet, heat a small amount of vegan butter over medium heat. It's important to preheat the pan before making your first pancake.
6. With a ½-cup measuring cup, scoop up some batter and pour it onto the preheated pan, using the cup to spread the batter and shape each pancake to the size you like. Once lots of bubbles begin to form on the pancakes and the bottoms are light brown, in 2 to 3 minutes, flip the pancakes over and cook the other side until light brown. Transfer to a plate. Repeat with the remaining batter until all the pancakes are cooked. Serve right away or freeze and reheat individual pancakes as you like (see Toni's tips).

TONI'S TIPS:

>>These pancakes freeze beautifully. Line a baking sheet with a silicone mat or parchment paper and lay the pancakes flat. Freeze for 1 hour, then store in a freezer bag or airtight container for up to 2 months. To reheat, microwave in 30-second increments to reach your desired temperature. No microwave? Reheat in the oven at 350 degrees for 10 minutes.

MY TIPS:

HASH BROWN VEGGIE BREAKFAST BURRITOS

Makes 8 burritos | Ready in 20 minutes

Honestly, you can wrap just about anything in a tortilla and it will taste better. Tofu scramble is no exception. With the help of hash browns, refried beans, peppers, and spices, I've put a Mexican-inspired twist on this hearty burrito, but you're welcome to change out this tofu scramble with the version from *The Friendly Vegan Cookbook,* or simply load up your tortilla with leftover cooked veggies, grains, or salad.

Ingredients:

2 cups frozen hash brown potatoes
1 tablespoon vegetable oil
½ large yellow or red onion, diced
½ large red or green bell pepper, diced
4–5 cremini or button mushrooms, sliced
3 garlic cloves, minced
1½ teaspoons ground cumin
¼ teaspoon ground turmeric
1 (14- to 16-ounce) package extra- or super-firm tofu, drained and pressed
Salt, to taste
8 burrito-size flour tortillas
1 (15-ounce) can vegetarian refried beans

Optional additions and swaps:

Swap the hash brown potatoes for tater tots
Swap the oil for ¼ cup water
For spice, add ½ teaspoon red chili flakes or 1 minced serrano pepper in step 2
For more flavor, add ⅛ teaspoon smoked paprika in step 3
For a cheesy flavor, add 1½ teaspoons nutritional yeast in step 3
Add crumbled cooked Soyrizo in step 6
Add vegan cheese in step 6

Optional additions for just before serving:

Diced avocado
Minced fresh cilantro
Pico de gallo (page 194)
Your favorite salsa or tomatillo salsa (page 188)

Directions:

1. Cook the hash brown potatoes according to the package instructions and set aside.

2. In a large skillet, heat the oil over medium-high heat. Add the onion, bell pepper, and mushrooms, and sauté until the bell pepper is tender, 3 to 4 minutes.
3. Stir in the garlic, cumin, and turmeric and cook until fragrant, about 1 minute.
4. Using your fingers, crumble the tofu into the pan and sauté until the tofu is golden, 4 to 6 minutes. Season with salt.
5. Warm the tortillas in the microwave for 15 seconds. (Alternatively, heat individual tortillas in another skillet over medium heat until warmed, about 1 minute.)
6. Slather a spoonful of refried beans onto each tortilla. Fill the tortillas with a generous scoop of the tofu filling and some hash brown potatoes. If you're serving your burritos right away, you can add avocado, cilantro, pico de gallo, and/or salsa now and roll them up. If you're freezing your burritos for later (see Toni's tips), it's best to add these ingredients after thawing.

TONI'S TIPS:

>>When frozen and reheated, these taste as fresh and delicious as the day they were made. After they've completely cooled, wrap each burrito individually in aluminum foil and place in a freezer bag or airtight container. Keep frozen for up to 2 months. To reheat, unwrap and microwave for 3 minutes, flip, and then heat for 3 more minutes. If you don't have a microwave, you can bake at 400 degrees for about 30 minutes, or until your burrito is heated through.

MY TIPS:

ONE-BOWL BREAKFAST BREAD

Makes 1 loaf | Ready in 1 hour 10 minutes

Whether you're hosting a weekend brunch or you're meal prepping for the work week, reach for this flexible recipe that can be customized to suit your taste and use whatever berries (or even veggies—think carrot or zucchini!) that you have on hand. I think it's delicious as it is, but check out my suggested additions for an extra boost of flavor and texture.

Ingredients:

½–¾ cup sugar
½ cup vegetable oil
⅓ cup unsweetened applesauce
1 teaspoon vanilla extract
1 cup shredded carrot or zucchini, *or* blueberries or raspberries
1½ cups all-purpose flour
1 teaspoon baking powder
¼ teaspoon salt

Optional additions:

Add ¼ cup old-fashioned oats in step 3
Add ¼ cup crushed walnuts or pecans in step 3
Add 1–2 teaspoons ground cinnamon in step 3

Directions:

1. Preheat the oven to 350 degrees. Lightly grease a standard loaf pan.
2. In a large bowl, mix together the sugar, oil, applesauce, and vanilla, as well as the shredded carrot or zucchini (if using).
3. Add the flour, baking powder, and salt and whisk until thoroughly combined. If you're using berries, fold them into the batter now.
4. Pour the batter into the prepared loaf pan. Bake for 50 to 55 minutes, until the loaf is golden brown and a toothpick inserted in the center comes out clean.

TONI'S TIPS:

>>This loaf freezes beautifully. Allow to cool completely, then throw it in a freezer bag or airtight container and freeze for up to 2 months. Or, to freeze individual slices for a grab-and-go breakfast, wrap individual pieces in aluminum foil, then freeze. To thaw, leave the (wrapped) loaf or slices on the counter overnight.

TESTERS' TIPS:

>>"I don't think gluten-free flour can be a substitute, as it makes it really gummy. If you want to make it gluten-free, try almond flour as a substitute."
—Micah J. from Germany

MY TIPS:

VEGAN BUTTERMILK BISCUITS

Makes 10 biscuits | Ready in 45 minutes

Candice C. from Buffalo, NY, one of the recipe testers for this book, says, "Nothing beats a biscuit fresh out of the oven with some butter and jam." She knows what she's talking about! These are tall and wonderfully fluffy, and the perfect base for your favorite spreads and toppings.

Ingredients:

6 tablespoons vegan butter

1 cup unsweetened plain plant-based milk

1 tablespoon apple cider vinegar

2¼ cups all-purpose flour, plus more for dusting

1½ tablespoons baking powder

1 tablespoon granulated sugar

½ teaspoon salt

Directions:

1. Put the vegan butter in tablespoon-chunks on a plate and chill in the freezer for 20 minutes.
2. In a glass liquid measuring cup or bowl, whisk together the plant-based milk and apple cider vinegar and allow to rest for 10 minutes. After 10 minutes on the counter, place in the refrigerator until ready to use.
3. Preheat the oven to 425 degrees. Line a rimmed baking sheet with a silicone baking mat or parchment paper.
4. In a large bowl, whisk together the flour, baking powder, sugar, and salt.
5. Add the frozen vegan butter to the dry flour mixture and use a fork or pastry cutter to mix it in until the mixture is crumbly.
6. Pour the milk mixture into the bowl and mix together by hand to form a rough dough. Be careful not to overmix.
7. Using your hands, spread out the dough into a rectangle about ¾ inch thick on a floured work surface. Fold it in half, fold it in half again, and then stretch it back out. Repeat this four times. If the dough is sticking, add a little more flour.
8. Spread the dough out about 1½ inches thick. Using a 2½- to 3-inch round cookie cutter, biscuit cutter, or cup, cut out biscuits and place

them on the prepared baking sheet. Gather the scraps, stretch it back out to 1½ inches thick, and cut more biscuits until all the dough is used.

9. Bake for 12 to 14 minutes, until lightly golden. Cool for 5 minutes before serving.

TONI'S TIPS:

>>These biscuits freeze beautifully. Allow them to cool completely, then toss them in a freezer bag or airtight container and freeze for up to 1 month. If you want to freeze them for longer, wrap the biscuits individually in aluminum foil before placing them in the container and they'll last up to 3 months. To thaw, either leave them (wrapped) on the counter before bed or microwave them for 30 seconds. If they need more time, try an additional 30 seconds.

MY TIPS:

EASIEST BANANA BREAKFAST MUFFINS

Makes 12 muffins | Ready in 35 minutes

These wholesome, flavorful muffins are my all-time favorite! We buy a lot of bananas in our home, and this is a fantastic way to use them when they're overripe. I love that these muffins are customizable, made with pantry staples I often already have on hand, and can be whipped together in 10 minutes.

Ingredients:

5 large ripe bananas
3 cups all-purpose flour
½ cup granulated sugar
2 teaspoons baking powder
2 teaspoons baking soda
1 teaspoon salt
⅔ cup vegetable oil or unsweetened applesauce
1¾ cups shredded carrot or zucchini, *or* blueberries or raspberries

Optional additions and swaps:

Swap the all-purpose flour for whole wheat flour or gluten-free flour
To omit or decrease the sugar, use very ripe bananas
Add 1–2 teaspoons ground cinnamon in step 3
Add ¼ cup crushed walnuts or pecans in step 4

Directions:

1. Preheat the oven to 375 degrees. Lightly grease a muffin tin or fill it with silicone or paper liners.
2. In a large bowl, mash the bananas.
3. Add the flour, sugar, baking powder, baking soda, salt, and vegetable oil or applesauce. Gently mix together until well combined.
4. Fold your choice of veggie or fruit into the batter.
5. Spoon the batter into the muffin tin, filling each cup to the top.
6. Bake for 25 minutes, or until the muffins are golden brown on top and a toothpick inserted in the center comes out clean.

TONI'S TIPS:

>>Good news: these muffins are freezer-friendly! Allow them to cool completely before tucking them into a freezer bag or airtight container, and they'll taste fresh-baked for up to 1 month. If you want to freeze them longer, wrap muffins individually in aluminum foil and they'll last up to 3 months. To thaw, either leave them (wrapped) on the counter before bed and enjoy in the morning, or unwrap and microwave for 30 seconds. If they still need more time, try an additional 30 seconds.

MY TIPS:

___

___

___

___

___

BAKED OATMEAL

Serves 8 to 9 | Ready in 1 hour

For an updated twist on your a.m. oatmeal, try baking it! This cooking method sets the oatmeal so it can even be cut into bars that are easier for eating on the go and freeze well for time-saving meal prep. Best of all is that it tastes just as good at room temperature as it does straight out of the oven.

Ingredients:

3 tablespoons flaxseed meal
¼ cup + 3½ tablespoons warm water
2 cups old-fashioned oats
½ cup your favorite chopped nuts
1½ teaspoons ground cinnamon
½ teaspoon salt
½ cup unsweetened applesauce
1 teaspoon vanilla extract
2½ tablespoons agave or maple syrup
1½ cups frozen or fresh blueberries

Optional additions and swaps:

Add 2 tablespoons unsweetened shredded coconut in step 3
Swap the blueberries for your favorite diced fruit
Swap half of the blueberries for ¾ cup dried fruit or vegan chocolate chips
Serve with a dollop of vegan yogurt

Directions:

1. Preheat the oven to 350 degrees. Line a 9-inch square baking pan with parchment paper.
2. In a small bowl, whisk together the flaxseed meal and warm water for 1 minute. Set aside for 5 minutes to thicken.
3. Combine the oats, nuts, cinnamon, and salt in the prepared pan and mix until well incorporated.
4. Pour in the applesauce, vanilla, flaxseed mixture, and agave or maple syrup and mix until well combined.
5. Gently stir in the blueberries.
6. Bake for 45 minutes, or until lightly golden, and serve warm. Store leftovers in an airtight container in the fridge for up to 1 week.

TONI'S TIPS:

>>Freezing this oatmeal for future on-the-go morning meals is a snap. Allow to cool completely, cut into squares, and store in a freezer bag or airtight container. You can thaw overnight on the counter, or loosely cover the bars with aluminum foil and bake at 350 degrees for 8 to 10 minutes, or microwave in 45-second increments.

MY TIPS:

10-MINUTE BREAKFAST QUINOA

Serves 2 to 4 | Ready in 10 minutes

When I'm feeling a little burnt out on oat-based recipes (it happens!), I turn to protein-packed quinoa to provide me with my morning sustenance. It's a great way to use up any leftover quinoa you have on hand. I love quinoa's wholesome flavor and slightly nutty texture.

Ingredients:

½–¾ cup plant-based milk
1 cup cooked quinoa
½ teaspoon ground cinnamon or pumpkin pie spice (store-bought or page 216)
½ cup your favorite mix-ins (berries, diced apple, diced sweet potato, dried cranberries, etc.)

Optional additions:

To make it sweeter, add ½–1 tablespoon brown sugar, agave, or maple syrup in step 2
Add a drop of vanilla extract in step 2
To make it moister, stir in 1–2 tablespoons plant-based milk when serving
Top with your favorite chopped nuts or seeds
Top with banana slices
Top with unsweetened shredded coconut

Directions:

1. In a small pot, bring the plant-based milk and quinoa to a simmer over medium heat.
2. Add the cinnamon and your chosen mix-ins, stir, cover, and let simmer until warmed all the way through, about 5 minutes.

TONI'S TIPS:

>>No precooked quinoa? No problem. To make on the stovetop, bring 2 cups plant-based milk to a boil over medium-high heat, then add 1 cup dry quinoa (rinsed). Reduce the heat to low, cover, and let the quinoa simmer for 15 minutes. Stir in your add-ins and cinnamon, cover, and cook until all the liquid has been absorbed, about 5 minutes more. Or, to save even more time, let your pressure cooker do all the work: Throw 2 cups plant-based milk, 1 cup dry quinoa (rinsed), and your mix-ins into the pot and cook on high pressure for 1 minute with a natural release. Voilà! Breakfast is served.

MY TIPS:

OVERNIGHT OATS (5 WAYS)

Weekday mornings sometimes feel rushed, so if I don't have an easy breakfast to wake up to, I tend to get overwhelmed and skip it altogether. This is suboptimal for a number of reasons, including the fact that I can get hangry without a morning meal! Having Overnight Oats on hand helps prevent that. I like to mix it up with different flavor combinations like PB&J (my favorite) and Chocolate Banana Nut. Sometimes I'll even eat them for dessert with a little dollop of coco whip. Yum!

CHOCOLATE BANANA NUT OVERNIGHT OATS

Serves 1 | Ready in 4 hours 10 minutes (10 minutes to prep, 4+ hours to chill)

Chocolate for breakfast? Absolutely! The nuts and banana add texture and protein, keeping you sated until lunchtime.

Ingredients:

¾ cup old-fashioned oats

½ large ripe banana, mashed

2 tablespoons cocoa powder

2 tablespoons crushed walnuts

½–1 tablespoon brown sugar (depending on your sweetness preference)

¾ cup plant-based milk

Optional additions:

Add another ¼ cup plant-based milk when serving

Directions:

1. Combine all the ingredients in a mason jar, bowl, or glass.
2. If you're using a mason jar, cover it and shake until mixed. If you're using another container, stir with a spoon until mixed.
3. Cover and refrigerate for at least 4 hours, or up to overnight.
4. When you wake up, mix and enjoy chilled. (No cooking or heating is necessary—the oats soften overnight.)

PEANUT BUTTER AND JELLY OVERNIGHT OATS

Serves 1 | Ready in 4 hours 10 minutes (10 minutes to prep, 4+ hours to chill)

Sandwiches aren't the only way to showcase this classic flavor combination. Try pairing them in your overnight oats for something new and equally tasty.

Ingredients:

¾ cup old-fashioned oats
¾ cup plant-based milk
2 tablespoons creamy peanut butter
2 tablespoons raspberry or strawberry preserves
Raspberries or chopped strawberries, for garnish
Crushed peanuts, for garnish

Optional additions:

Add 1–2 teaspoons chia seeds in step 1
Add 1 teaspoon agave or maple syrup in step 1

Directions:

1. Combine the oats and milk in a mason jar, bowl, or glass.
2. In a small microwave-safe bowl, microwave the peanut butter for 30 seconds. Mix with a fork until smooth. (If the peanut butter is still lumpy, microwave in 20-second increments, mixing in between, until it's completely smooth.)
3. Pour the melted peanut butter over the oat mixture. Top with the preserves.
4. Cover and refrigerate for at least 4 hours, or up to overnight.
5. In the morning, mix and garnish with fruit and crushed peanuts. Enjoy chilled. (No cooking or heating is necessary—the oats soften overnight.)

TONI'S TIP:

>>Homemade plant-based milk is often more affordable (and less wasteful) than store-bought. What I like about cashew milk above all others is that it uses the entire nut, retaining 100 percent of the fiber. No need to strain or buy a nut-milk bag! Make your own Cashew Milk at home by combining 1 cup raw cashews (soaked overnight, then drained and rinsed), 4 cups water, 1–2 tablespoons maple syrup or agave, 1 teaspoon vanilla extract, and a pinch of salt in a high-powered blender. Blend on high for 2 minutes, or until completely creamy. (If you're using a standard blender, you'll need to blend for 5 or 6 minutes to achieve the right consistency.)

APPLE CINNAMON OVERNIGHT OATS

Serves 1 | Ready in 4 hours 10 minutes (10 minutes to prep, 4+ hours to chill)

Maybe you used to buy those little packets of apple cinnamon instant oatmeal, and still occasionally crave those wholesome flavors. This is an updated version that tastes similar but is even healthier!

Ingredients:

¾ cup old-fashioned oats
¼ cup diced apple, your choice on the variety
2 tablespoons chopped walnuts
½ teaspoon ground cinnamon
1 cup plant-based milk
1½ teaspoons maple syrup or agave

Optional additions and swaps:

Swap the walnuts for pecans or other nuts
Swap the cinnamon for apple pie spice or pumpkin pie spice (store-bought or page 216)
Swap the maple syrup or agave for brown sugar
Add ¼ teaspoon vanilla extract in step 1

Directions:

1. Combine all the ingredients in a mason jar, bowl or glass.
2. If you're using a mason jar, cover it and shake until mixed. If you're using another container, stir with a spoon until mixed.
3. Cover and refrigerate for at least 4 hours, or up to overnight.
4. When you wake up, mix and enjoy chilled. (No cooking or heating is necessary—the oats soften overnight.)

TESTERS' TIPS:

>>"A spoonful of peanut butter on top would just make this absolutely heavenly."
—Melanie S. from Warsaw, NY

CHIA BLUEBERRY OVERNIGHT OATS

Serves 1 | Ready in 4 hours 10 minutes (10 minutes to prep, 4+ hours to chill)

Chia seeds and blueberries are superfoods that will give you a revitalizing boost on busy mornings. Try topping yours with toasted nuts or seeds for extra protein and a satisfying crunch.

Ingredients:

¾ cup old-fashioned oats
¼ cup frozen blueberries
2 tablespoons raw sunflower seeds
1 teaspoon chia seeds
½ teaspoon ground cinnamon
1 cup plant-based milk
1½ teaspoons maple syrup or agave

Optional additions and swaps:

Swap the cinnamon for apple pie spice or pumpkin pie spice (store-bought or page 216)
Swap the sunflower seeds for pumpkin seeds or chopped nuts
Swap the chia seeds for flaxmeal
Swap the maple syrup or agave for brown sugar
Add ¼ teaspoon vanilla extract in step 1

Directions:

1. Combine all the ingredients in a mason jar, bowl, or glass.
2. If you're using a mason jar, cover it and shake until mixed. If you're using another container, stir with a spoon until mixed.
3. Cover and refrigerate for at least 4 hours, or up to overnight.
4. When you wake up, mix and enjoy chilled. (No cooking or heating is necessary—the oats soften overnight.)

PUMPKIN PIE OVERNIGHT OATS

Serves 1 | Ready in 4 hours 10 minutes (10 minutes to prep, 4+ hours to chill)

If you're a pumpkin pie fan, you'll love this version of Overnight Oats. Best of all is that you don't have to wait for the holidays to enjoy them. I eat them for breakfast all year round!

Ingredients:

¾ cup old-fashioned oats
¼ cup canned pumpkin purée
¼ teaspoon pumpkin pie spice (store-bought or page 216)
1 cup plant-based milk
1½ teaspoons maple syrup or agave (optional)

Optional additions:

Garnish with pumpkin seeds
Add ¼ teaspoon vanilla extract in step 1

Directions:

1. Combine all the ingredients in a mason jar, bowl, or glass.
2. If you're using a mason jar, cover it and shake until mixed. If you're using another container, stir with a spoon until mixed.
3. Cover and refrigerate for at least 4 hours, or up to overnight.
4. When you wake up, mix and enjoy chilled. (No cooking or heating is necessary—the oats soften overnight.)

MY TIPS:

SMOOTHIE FREEZER PACKS (5 WAYS)

Everyone knows that smoothies make for a quick, healthy breakfast option, but I like to streamline the process even further by creating ready-to-roll smoothie packs in reusable bags or containers with all the fixings (minus your preferred blending liquid). On busy mornings, just dump the contents of your smoothie pack into a blender, blend with your liquid, and boom! You're ready to head out the door! These are all simple smoothie bases that allow you to customize with your favorite mix-ins.

PEACH OJ SMOOTHIE PACK

Serves 1 | Ready in 5 minutes

This smoothie tastes like sunshine in a glass. Frozen peaches are convenient and allow you to enjoy this all year round, but fresh, in-season peaches work just as well.

Ingredients:

1½ cups frozen peach slices
½ cup raspberries
1½ cups orange juice

Optional additions:

Add ¾ cup spinach or kale in step 1
Add 1½ teaspoons flaxseed meal or chia seeds in step 1
Add 3 tablespoons vanilla protein powder in step 1
For a creamier smoothie, add a 5.3-ounce container vegan vanilla yogurt in step 2

Directions:

1. Seal the peaches and raspberries in a freezer bag, airtight container, or mason jar, and place in the freezer until you're ready to use.
2. When you're ready for a smoothie, empty your smoothie packet into the blender, add the orange juice, and blend until smooth.

MANGO-PINEAPPLE SMOOTHIE PACK

Serves 1 | Ready in 5 minutes

For those days when you're dreaming of a tropical vacation, this thick and luscious smoothie will take you there!

Ingredients:

1 cup frozen mango slices
½ cup frozen pineapple chunks
½ large banana, cut into chunks, frozen
1½ cups plant-based milk

Optional additions:

Add ¼ cup unsweetened shredded coconut in step 1
Add 3 tablespoons vanilla protein powder in step 1
For a sweeter smoothie, add 1½ teaspoons maple syrup or agave in step 2

Directions:

1. Seal the mango, pineapple, and banana in a freezer bag, airtight container, or mason jar, and place in the freezer until you're ready to use.
2. When you're ready for a smoothie, empty your smoothie packet into the blender, add the milk, and blend until smooth.

MIXED BERRY SMOOTHIE PACK

Serves 1 | Ready in 5 minutes

This smoothie is endlessly customizable. Try it with just one type of berry, such as strawberries or blackberries, or toss a variety together for a more complex flavor.

Ingredients:

1½ cups your favorite fresh or frozen mixed berries
¼ cup packed spinach
1½ teaspoons flaxseed meal
¼ teaspoon ground cinnamon
1½ cups plant-based milk

Optional additions:

Add 3 tablespoons vanilla protein powder in step 1
For a sweeter smoothie, add 1½ teaspoons maple syrup or agave in step 2
Add a dash of vanilla extract in step 2

Directions:

1. Seal the berries, spinach, flaxseed meal, and cinnamon in a freezer bag, airtight container, or mason jar, and place in the freezer until you're ready to use.
2. When you're ready for a smoothie, empty your smoothie packet into the blender, add the milk, and blend until smooth.

BLUEBERRY KALE SMOOTHIE PACK

Serves 1 | Ready in 5 minutes

Blueberries are bursting with antioxidants, and kale is a good source of vitamin A and potassium, making this the ultimate superfood smoothie!

Ingredients:

1 large banana, cut into chunks, frozen
1 cup fresh or frozen blueberries
¾ cup packed fresh kale
1 cup plant-based milk

Optional additions and swaps:

Swap the kale for spinach
Add 1½ teaspoons flaxseed meal in step 1
Add 3 tablespoons vanilla protein powder in step 1

Directions:

1. Seal the banana, blueberries, and kale in a freezer bag, airtight container, or mason jar, and place in the freezer until you're ready to use.
2. When you're ready for a smoothie, empty your smoothie packet into the blender, add the milk, and blend until smooth.

CHERRY BANANA SMOOTHIE PACK

Serves 1 | Ready in 5 minutes

The secret ingredient to this thick and fruity blend is protein-rich peanut butter, which makes you feel sated long after you've sipped the last of your smoothie.

Ingredients:

- 1 cup frozen cherries
- 1 large banana, cut into chunks, frozen
- 1 tablespoon peanut butter
- 1 teaspoon cocoa powder
- ½–¾ cup plant-based milk

Directions:

1. Seal the cherries, banana, peanut butter, and cocoa powder in a freezer bag, airtight container, or mason jar, and place in the freezer until you're ready to use.
2. When you're ready for a smoothie, empty your smoothie packet into the blender, add the milk (starting with ½ cup), and blend until smooth. If you'd like a thinner smoothie, add the rest of the milk.

TONI'S TIPS:

>>If you're using a standard blender (instead of a high-speed blender), start blending the milk with just ¼ cup of the cherries, then slowly add the rest of the ingredients as you go. It'll be easier on your blender.

MY TIPS:

ONE-POT MEALS

One-pot meals are the best—especially for people like me who dread kitchen cleanup! Besides the ease of preparation and having fewer dishes to wash, cooking an entire meal in one pot encourages me to get creative with ingredients and make delicious meals that are simple to pull together but complex in flavor. Here are some of my favorites.

SOPA DE FIDEO

Serves 4 | Ready in 20 minutes

Sopa de Fideo, also called Sopita by my family, is a soup that my grandma used to make for me when I was little, and sitting down to a steaming bowlful still feels like being wrapped in one of her hugs. Traditionally, the broth is made by blending fresh Roma tomatoes, but I use canned tomato sauce because I learned to make it that way—and because I don't want to have to wash the blender! I then stir in a couple of diced fresh tomatoes for extra flavor and texture.

Ingredients:

1 tablespoon vegetable oil
½ medium yellow onion, diced
3 medium garlic cloves, minced
1 small zucchini, diced
1 (7-ounce) package fideo pasta
2 Roma tomatoes, diced
1½ teaspoons ground cumin
5 cups vegetable broth
1 (8-ounce) can tomato sauce

Optional additions and swaps:

Swap the oil for ¼ cup water
Add salt to taste in step 2
Add 1 cup extra vegetable broth if you want it soupier
Stir in 1 cup cooked or canned black or pinto beans after step 3

Directions:

1. In a medium saucepan, heat the oil over medium-high heat. Sauté the onion and garlic for 1 minute. Add the zucchini and fideo noodles and sauté until the noodles turn very light brown, 1 to 2 minutes.
2. Add the tomatoes, cumin, broth, and tomato sauce and stir until thoroughly combined.
3. Bring to a boil, cover with a lid, reduce the heat to low, and let simmer until the noodles have softened, about 10 minutes.

TONI'S TIPS:

>>If you can't find fideo pasta at your local grocery store (look for it in the Hispanic foods section), you can use angel hair pasta broken up into 1-inch pieces.

MY TIPS:

VEGGIE-PACKED POTATO LEEK SOUP

Serves 4 to 6 | Ready in 30 minutes

This delicious and comforting soup is the perfect recipe for putting all the odds and ends lurking in your fridge's veggie drawer to good use. Puréeing the vegetables after they've simmered gives it a velvety texture that tastes ultra creamy, with no cream required.

Ingredients:

2 tablespoons vegetable oil
1 small yellow or red onion, diced
4 garlic cloves, minced
3 carrots, thinly sliced
3 celery stalks, sliced
1 large zucchini, sliced and halved
3 leeks, sliced (using mostly the white part)
8 cups vegetable or "No Chicken" broth
3 pounds scrubbed and chopped russet potatoes
½–1 teaspoon salt
Black pepper, to taste

Optional additions and swaps:

Swap the vegetable oil for ½ cup water
For a deeper flavor, add any of these in step 2: 2 bay leaves (remove before puréeing), ½ teaspoon dried thyme, ½ teaspoon garlic powder, ½ teaspoon onion powder
For a tangy flavor, add the juice of 1 small lemon when serving
For spice, add a dash of sriracha when serving
For protein, add 1 (15-ounce) can garbanzo beans, drained and rinsed (1½ cups), after step 3 and cook for a few additional minutes to heat through

Directions:

1. In a large soup pot, heat the oil over medium-high heat. Add the onion, garlic, carrots, celery, zucchini, and leeks, and cook until the veggies are tender, about 5 minutes.
2. Add the broth and potatoes and bring to a boil. Boil until the potatoes are cooked all the way through, 10 to 15 minutes.
3. Remove from the heat. Purée half of the soup using an immersion blender (or with a regular blender, working in batches). If working in batches, return the puréed soup to the pot and combine with the remaining soup. Season with salt and black pepper.

TONI'S TIPS:

>> If you have a pressure cooker, this scrumptious soup can be on the table in less than 10 minutes! Just throw everything in (feel free to leave out the oil) and cook on high pressure for 5 minutes with a quick release. Then continue to step 3.

When completely cooled, this soup can be stored in an airtight container (filled only three-quarters of the way to allow for expansion) and frozen for up to 5 months. To reheat, thaw in the refrigerator overnight, then heat it on the stovetop or in a microwave.

MY TIPS:

____

____

____

____

CURRIED LENTIL SOUP

Serves 4 to 6 | Ready in 30 minutes

This easy one-pot dish is rich and filling thanks to the addition of coconut milk, and it makes the perfect warming antidote to a cold day. Best of all is that it's ready to eat in just 30 minutes, making it ideal for busy weeknight meals.

Ingredients:

1 tablespoon vegetable oil
1 small yellow or red onion, diced
1 red or green bell pepper, diced
1 tablespoon minced ginger
3 garlic cloves, minced
2 small carrots, sliced
2 celery ribs, sliced
1 tablespoon curry powder
1½ cups red lentils
4 cups water
1 (13.5-ounce) can coconut milk
2 vegetable bouillon cubes or "No Chicken" paste equivalent
Salt and black pepper, to taste

Optional additions and swaps:

Swap the oil for ¼ cup vegetable broth
For a heartier soup, add 1 cup of any diced vegetables in step 1
For spice, add ½–1 teaspoon red chili flakes in step 1
For more texture and protein, add 1 (15-ounce) can garbanzo beans, drained and rinsed (1½ cups), in step 2
Add 1 (14-ounce) can regular or fire-roasted diced tomatoes and their juices in step 2
Don't have coconut milk? Swap in more vegetable broth
Garnish with a drizzle of additional coconut milk

Directions:

1. In a large pot, heat the oil over medium-high heat. Add the onion, bell pepper, ginger, garlic, carrots, celery, and curry powder and sauté until the onion becomes tender, 3 to 4 minutes.
2. Pour in the lentils, water, coconut milk, and bouillon cubes. Bring to a boil, cover, lower the heat, and simmer until the lentils are tender, 15 to 20 minutes. Season with salt and pepper.

TESTERS' TIPS:

>>"To make it Thai-style, add a tablespoon of Thai red curry paste and coconut milk. For high protein and lower fat, replace the coconut milk with veggie broth and add the optional garbanzo beans." —Yiran L. from Boulder, CO

TONI'S TIPS:

>>For a wholesome meal in no time flat, make this in a pressure cooker. Simply throw everything into the pressure cooker (omitting the oil) and cook on high pressure for 5 minutes with a quick release.

When completely cooled, this soup can be stored in an airtight container (filled only three-quarters of the way to allow for expansion) and frozen for up to 5 months. To reheat, thaw in the refrigerator overnight, then heat it on the stovetop or in a microwave.

MY TIPS:

___

___

___

___

MUSHROOM AND WHITE BEAN SOUP

Serves 4 to 6 | Ready in 30 minutes

This Italian-style soup is hearty and irresistible, and the surprise addition of quinoa makes it extra filling. Serve it with a salad and some crusty bread for the ultimate comfort-food feast.

Ingredients:

1 tablespoon vegetable oil
1 small yellow or red onion, diced
2 large carrots, sliced
8 ounces cremini or button mushrooms, sliced
3 garlic cloves, minced
1½ teaspoons Italian seasoning (store-bought or see Toni's Tips below)
2 (15-ounce) cans cannellini beans, drained and rinsed
⅔ cup quinoa
7 cups vegetable or "No Chicken" broth
1 bunch spinach, optionally stemmed and chopped
Black pepper, to taste

Optional additions and swaps:

To save time, use a cup or two of baby carrots instead of slicing large carrots
For more flavor, add 1 teaspoon garlic powder + 1 teaspoon onion powder in step 2
For more heartiness, add a (14.5-ounce) can diced tomatoes, drained, in step 3
Swap the cannellini beans for your choice of beans
Swap the spinach for kale
For some spice, add red chili flakes, sriracha, or your favorite hot sauce when serving

Directions:

1. In a large pot, heat the oil over medium-high heat. Add the onion, carrots, mushrooms, and garlic and sauté until the onion is tender and translucent, about 3 minutes. Stir in the Italian seasoning and sauté for 1 more minute.
2. Pour in the beans, quinoa, and vegetable broth. Bring to a boil, then cover and reduce the heat to medium-low. Simmer for 10 minutes.
3. Stir in the spinach, cover, and cook until the spinach has wilted and the quinoa is soft, about 10 minutes. Season with a few grinds of pepper.

TONI'S TIPS:

>>Surprise! This soup works great in the pressure cooker. Throw everything but the spinach into the pot, omitting the oil if you prefer, and cook on high pressure for 5 minutes with a quick release. Stir in the spinach while it's still piping hot for perfectly cooked greens.

When completely cooled, this soup can be stored in an airtight container (filled only three-quarters of the way to allow for expansion) and frozen for up to 5 months. To reheat, thaw in the refrigerator overnight, then heat it on the stovetop or in a microwave.

If you don't have premade Italian seasoning, you can DIY. In a small jar, combine 1½ teaspoons dried basil, 1½ teaspoons dried oregano, 1 teaspoon dried marjoram, ½ teaspoon dried thyme, ½ teaspoon dried rosemary, and ¼ teaspoon garlic powder. Store in a cool, dry place until you're ready to use it.

MY TIPS:

CALDO DE TOFU

Serves 6 | Ready in 45 minutes

Of all the recipes in this book, this savory dish is the one I make the most often, not just because it's delicious, but because it connects me to my past. Throughout childhood, my grandma would make me various versions of this soup, and as an adult, it brings me so much comfort to make it and share it with others. Expect a vegan, Mexican-inspired twist on a Chicken and Rice Soup with tofu swapped in for the chicken and with the addition of fresh lemon juice and cilantro. So delicious!

Ingredients:

1 tablespoon vegetable oil
1 medium yellow onion, thinly sliced
3 carrots, sliced
3 celery ribs, sliced
2 medium zucchini, diced
3 garlic cloves, minced
2 ears corn, shucked and cut into thirds
1 (14- to 16-ounce) package extra- or super-firm tofu, drained and diced
¾ cup medium-grain white rice, rinsed
6 cups water
3 vegetable bouillon cubes or "No Chicken" paste equivalent
Salt and black pepper, to taste
Minced fresh cilantro, for garnish

Optional additions and swaps:

Swap the oil for ¼ cup water
Swap the rice for quinoa
Add a squeeze of lemon or lime juice before serving
Add a dash of hot sauce before serving
Add sliced jalapeños before serving

Directions:

1. In a large pot, heat the oil over medium heat. Add the onion, carrots, celery, zucchini, and garlic and sauté, stirring frequently, until the vegetables are tender, 3 to 5 minutes.
2. Add the corn, tofu, rice, water, and bouillon cubes. Bring to a boil, cover, and lower the heat, and simmer for 25 minutes. Season with salt and pepper. Garnish with minced cilantro.

TONI'S TIPS:

>>If you guessed that this soup can be made in a pressure cooker, you'd be right! Combine all the ingredients in the pressure cooker (omitting the oil if you like) and cook on high pressure for 4 minutes with a quick release.

MY TIPS:

LENTIL VEGETABLE STEW

Serves 4 to 6 | Ready in 45 minutes

For time-saving meal prep, there's no better one-pot meal than this hearty stew, brimming with flavor and texture. Keeping the base recipe simple leaves plenty of room for customizing with different add-ins throughout the week.

Ingredients:

1 tablespoon vegetable oil
1 small onion, diced
3 garlic cloves, minced
1 small zucchini, halved and sliced
3 small carrots, sliced
2 celery ribs, sliced
1 small sweet potato, scrubbed and diced
1 (15-ounce) can garbanzo beans, drained and rinsed
½ cup quinoa
¾ cup brown lentils
6 cups water
3 vegetable bouillon cubes or "No Chicken" paste equivalent
Salt and black pepper, to taste

Optional additions and swaps:

Swap the oil for ¼–½ cup water
Swap any vegetable for another fresh or frozen vegetable of your choice
Swap the garbanzo beans for another bean of your choice
Swap the brown lentils for green lentils
For more flavor, add 2 bay leaves in step 2 (remove before serving)
For more flavor, add 1 teaspoon dried thyme in step 2
Add a squeeze of lemon juice when serving
Add a dash of hot sauce when serving
Garnish with minced fresh parsley or cilantro when serving

Directions:

1. In a large pot, heat the oil over medium-high heat. Add the onion, garlic, zucchini, carrots, celery, and sweet potato and sauté until the onion is tender and translucent, about 3 minutes.
2. Add the garbanzo beans, quinoa, lentils, and broth. Bring to a boil, cover, reduce the heat to low, and simmer for 30 minutes. Season with salt and pepper.

TONI'S TIPS:

>>Cooking this stew in a pressure cooker reduces the cooking time from 30 minutes to less than 10! Just throw everything into the pressure cooker and cook on high pressure for 8 minutes with a quick release.

This soup can be stored in an airtight container in the refrigerator for up to 5 days or in the freezer (with the container filled only three-quarters of the way to allow for expansion) for up to 5 months. To reheat, thaw in the refrigerator overnight, then heat it on the stovetop or in a microwave.

MY TIPS:

SIMPLE BLACK BEAN CHILI

Serves 6 | Ready in 30 minutes

This Black Bean Chili is a versatile, comforting, and nutrient-packed meal that you can get on the table in under 30 minutes. I love how filling and customizable it is. Plus, it's easy to prepare and delicious to eat. Win-win-win!

Ingredients:

1 tablespoon vegetable oil
1 small yellow or red onion, diced
1 green or red bell pepper, diced
3 garlic cloves, minced
4 (15-ounce) cans black beans, drained and rinsed
2 (14.5-ounce) cans diced tomatoes, with their juices
1 (15.25-ounce) can corn kernels, drained
1 tablespoon chili powder
2 teaspoons ground cumin
½–1 teaspoon salt

Optional additions and swaps:

Swap the oil for ¼ cup water or vegetable broth
Swap the black beans for any beans you like
Swap the canned corn for 1½ cups frozen corn
If you like it spicy, add 1 teaspoon cayenne pepper, red chili flakes, or minced jalapeño in step 2
For more flavor, add 1 teaspoon each garlic powder and onion powder in step 2
Garnish with chopped fresh cilantro
Top with sliced avocado
Top with minced onion
Add a squeeze of lime juice when serving

Directions:

1. In a large pot, heat the oil over medium-high heat. Add the onion, bell pepper, and garlic and sauté until the veggies are tender and the onion is translucent, 3 to 5 minutes.
2. Add the beans, tomatoes and their juices, corn, chili powder, cumin, and salt. Stir to combine and let the mixture come to a simmer, then lower the heat to medium-low, cover, and cook, stirring occasionally, for 15 minutes.

TONI'S TIPS:

>>Beans and pressure cookers are a match made in culinary heaven. Simply toss everything into the pressure cooker and cook on high pressure for 3 minutes, then use a quick release.

When completely cooled, this chili can be stored in one or more airtight containers and frozen for up to 3 months. To reheat, thaw in the refrigerator overnight, then heat it on the stovetop or in a microwave.

MY TIPS:

____

____

____

____

CREAMY ASPARAGUS SOUP

Serves 4 to 6 | Ready in 45 minutes

When asparagus season arrives, this soup is in regular rotation at my house. I love its simplicity, and despite its delicate flavor, it's surprisingly filling. Try switching it up by varying the consistency—giving it just a few pulses for a chunkier version one time, then puréeing until completely smooth the next (or with any leftovers).

Ingredients:

1 tablespoon vegetable oil
1 small yellow, red, or white onion, diced
6 small garlic cloves, minced
3–4 pounds russet potatoes, chopped
1 (15-ounce) can cannellini beans, drained and rinsed
7 cups vegetable or "No Chicken" broth
1 pound asparagus, cut into 1-inch pieces
Juice of ½–1 lemon
Salt and black pepper, to taste

Optional additions and swaps:

Swap the oil for ¼ cup water or vegetable broth
Add a 1-inch piece fresh ginger, minced, in step 1
For more flavor, add 1 teaspoon garlic powder + 1 teaspoon onion powder in step 2
Swap the cannellini beans for any other white beans

Directions:

1. In a large pot, heat the oil over medium heat. Add the onion and garlic and sauté until the onion becomes tender and translucent, about 5 minutes.
2. Add the potatoes, beans, and vegetable broth. Turn the heat to high, bring to a boil, and boil until the potatoes are cooked all the way through, about 15 minutes. If it starts boiling too heavily, turn the heat down to medium-high.
3. Add the asparagus and cook until the asparagus is softened, about 5 minutes.
4. Remove from the heat. Purée half of the soup using an immersion blender (or with a regular blender, working in batches). If working in batches, return the puréed soup to the pot and combine it with the remaining soup. Add the lemon juice and season with salt and pepper.

TONI'S TIPS:

>>If you want to make this in your pressure cooker, combine all the ingredients in the pressure cooker (omitting the oil) and cook on high pressure for 5 minutes with a quick release, then continue to step 4.

When completely cooled, this soup can be stored in an airtight container (filled only three-quarters of the way to allow for expansion) and frozen for up to 3 months. To reheat, thaw in the refrigerator overnight, then heat it on the stovetop or in a microwave.

MY TIPS:

___

___

___

ITALIAN-INSPIRED SOUP

Serves 4 to 6 | **Ready in 30 minutes**

This is a throw-in-everything-but-the-kitchen-sink take on a classic minestrone: fresh vegetables, pasta, and beans swimming in a flavorful tomato broth. To amp up the Italian vibes, serve it with some crusty bread dipped in a fruity olive oil.

Ingredients:

1 tablespoon vegetable oil
1 small yellow or red onion, diced
2 carrots, sliced
2 celery ribs, sliced
1 large russet potato, scrubbed and diced
5 garlic cloves, minced
1½ tablespoons Italian seasoning (store-bought or page 62)
8 cups vegetable or "No Chicken" broth
1 (15-ounce) can garbanzo beans, drained and rinsed
1 (14.5-ounce) can diced tomatoes, with their juices
1 cup your favorite pasta
Black pepper, to taste

Optional additions and swaps:

Swap the vegetable oil for ½ cup water
Swap the russet potato for sweet potato or any potato variety
For an even heartier soup, add 1 cup fresh or frozen vegetables (sliced mushrooms, peas, broccoli florets, etc.) in step 2
For more flavor, stir in ¼ cup packed sliced fresh basil after step 3
For more acidity, add a squeeze of lemon juice when serving
For more spice, add a splash of hot sauce when serving

Directions:

1. In a large pot, heat the oil over medium-high heat. Add the onion, carrots, celery, potato, garlic, and Italian seasoning, and sauté until the onion becomes tender and translucent, 3 to 4 minutes.
2. Stir in the broth, garbanzo beans, and tomatoes and their juices. Bring to a boil, then lower the heat and simmer for 5 minutes.
3. Add the pasta and continue to cook until tender according to the pasta package instructions. Season with a few grinds of pepper.

TONI'S TIPS:

>>The pressure cooker's magic can easily be applied to this soup. Combine all of the ingredients in the pot (omitting the oil if you like) and cook on high pressure for 3 minutes with a quick release.

When completely cooled, this soup can be stored in an airtight container (filled only three-quarters of the way to allow for expansion) and frozen for up to 5 months. To reheat, thaw in the refrigerator overnight, then heat it on the stovetop or in a microwave.

MY TIPS:

RED CURRY WITH TOFU AND VEGETABLES

Serves 4 to 6 | **Ready in 35 minutes**

Red curry paste from a jar helps this meal come together quickly and deliciously. (Check the ingredients to make sure there's no shrimp paste lurking inside. My favorite vegan-friendly brand is Thai Kitchen.) Like most dishes in this chapter, this curry is customizable; add your favorite vegetables to make it a weeknight meal tailored to your tastes and whatever's in season.

Ingredients:

1 tablespoon vegetable oil
1 small yellow onion, sliced
1 (4-ounce) jar red curry paste
7 cups your favorite chopped vegetables (bell pepper, broccoli florets, zucchini, carrots, potatoes, etc.)
2 (13.5-ounce) cans full-fat coconut milk
1 teaspoon brown sugar
½ teaspoon salt
1 (14- to 16-ounce) package extra- or super-firm tofu, drained and diced

Optional additions and swaps:

Swap the oil for ¼ cup water
For spice and flavor, add a pinch of red chili flakes to each bowl as a garnish when serving
For more protein, add 1 (15-ounce) can garbanzo beans, drained and rinsed (1½ cups), in step 2
Swap the red curry paste for yellow curry paste
Serve with steamed brown or white rice
Garnish with crushed peanuts

Directions:

1. In a large pot, heat the oil over medium-high heat. Add the onion and sauté until tender and translucent, 2 to 3 minutes.
2. Add the curry paste, vegetables, coconut milk, brown sugar, salt, and tofu, and stir everything together.
3. Bring to a boil, then cover, lower the heat to low, and cook until your vegetables are cooked to your liking, 15 to 20 minutes.

TONI'S TIPS:

>>When completely cooled, this curry can be stored in one or more airtight containers and frozen for up to 3 months. To reheat, thaw in the refrigerator overnight, then heat it on the stovetop or in a microwave.

MY TIPS:

TURMERIC VEGGIES AND YELLOW SPLIT PEAS

Serves 4 to 6 | Ready in 45 minutes

Before we were married, my husband lived in Silver Spring, Maryland, home to a vibrant Ethiopian community and some truly amazing Ethiopian restaurants. Back then, most of our date nights were spent enjoying the flavorful East African cuisine, inspiring me to explore new flavors in my own kitchen. This dish (though in no way intended to be authentic!) is inspired by kik alicha, a popular Ethiopian dish made with turmeric and yellow split peas.

Ingredients:

1½ tablespoons vegetable or olive oil
1 small yellow onion, diced
5 garlic cloves, minced
1 (1-inch) piece ginger, minced
1 jalapeño, minced
1 small head broccoli, chopped
1 medium zucchini, diced
1 cup yellow split peas
2¾ cups vegetable broth
½ teaspoon ground turmeric
½ teaspoon salt

Optional additions and swaps:

Swap the oil for ¼–½ cup vegetable broth
Swap the broccoli for 1½ cups another chopped vegetable
Swap zucchini for 1 cup another chopped vegetable
For a cheesy flavor, add 2 tablespoons nutritional yeast in step 3
Serve over steamed brown rice or quinoa
Add salt to taste when serving

Directions:

1. In a large pot, heat the oil over medium-high heat. Add the onion and sauté until tender and translucent, about 5 minutes.
2. Add the garlic, ginger, and jalapeño, and cook for another 1 to 2 minutes.
3. Add the broccoli, zucchini, split peas, vegetable broth, turmeric, and salt. Bring to a boil, then cover, lower the heat, and simmer for 30 minutes. If there's still broth in the pot when you remove the lid, turn up the heat and stir continuously until the broth evaporates and the stew thickens.

MY TIPS:

MEAL PREP PASTA SALAD

Serves 4 to 6 | Ready in 50 minutes (20 minutes to prep, 30 minutes to chill)

This colorful, veggie-packed pasta salad is a stellar make-ahead lunch option for the week, as the flavors continue to improve with each day! The beans and olives add heartiness, so you'll be satiated straight through until dinnertime.

Ingredients:

1 (1-pound) package your favorite pasta
1 (15-ounce) can garbanzo beans, drained and rinsed
1 small cucumber, diced
1½ cups halved cherry tomatoes
½ small red or yellow onion, diced
½ cup minced fresh curly parsley
1 (2.25-ounce) can sliced black olives, drained
¼ cup balsamic vinegar
¼ cup lemon juice
2 tablespoons olive oil
Salt and black pepper, to taste

Optional swaps:

Omit the oil
Swap the black olives for ½ cup other olive varieties

Directions:

1. In a large pot, cook the pasta according to the package instructions until tender. Drain.
2. While the pasta cooks, combine the remaining ingredients in a large bowl and mix them together.
3. Add the cooked pasta and thoroughly combine. Allow to chill in the refrigerator for at least 30 minutes before serving.
4. For meal prepping, divide the pasta salad into airtight containers in individual servings and store in the refrigerator for up to 5 days.

MY TIPS:

PASTA O'S

Serves 2 to 4 | Ready in 10 minutes

I grew up eating canned SpaghettiOs and was a little heartbroken to say goodbye to them when I became vegan. What I didn't know then was that I could easily whip up a perfect copycat (minus the dairy and high-fructose corn syrup) in just minutes!

Ingredients:

1 (7-ounce) package uncooked O-shaped pasta, alphabet pasta, or star pasta
2 (8-ounce) cans tomato sauce
3 tablespoons vegan butter
2½ tablespoons nutritional yeast
1½ teaspoons granulated sugar
½ teaspoon onion powder
¼ teaspoon salt

Optional additions:

For more spice, add ⅛ teaspoon paprika in step 2
For more acidity, add ⅛ teaspoon apple cider vinegar in step 2
For sweeter pasta, add ¼ teaspoon more granulated sugar in step 2

Directions:

1. In a medium saucepan, cook the pasta according to the package instructions. Drain the pasta and return it to the pot.
2. Stir in the tomato sauce, butter, nutritional yeast, sugar, onion powder, and salt and let the residual heat from the pot melt the butter and warm everything through. Taste and adjust the seasoning as you like.

TONI'S TIPS:

>>Alphabet and star-shaped pasta is often found in the Hispanic foods section of the grocery store.

MY TIPS:

TABBOULEH-INSPIRED QUINOA

Serves 2 to 4 | Ready in 40 minutes (20 minutes to cook, 20 minutes to cool)

Fast-cooking quinoa is the perfect blank canvas for summer salads. I'm lucky enough to have a garden, and in peak season, I love to use just-harvested veggies to add extra flavor to this simple, fresh, and wholesome dish inspired by the Middle Eastern classic. Using protein-rich quinoa instead of the usual bulgur wheat makes this satisfying enough to enjoy as a light meal, and it's perfect for meal prepping.

Ingredients:

1 cup quinoa
1¾ cups vegetable broth
1 small cucumber, diced
1 large tomato, diced
1 cup chopped fresh curly parsley
¼ cup chopped fresh mint
2 garlic cloves, minced
2 tablespoons lemon juice

Optional additions:

For more flavor, add ½ teaspoon garlic powder + ½ teaspoon onion powder in step 1
For more heartiness, add 1 cup sliced olives in step 3
For more protein, add 1 cup cooked or canned garbanzo beans in step 3
Garnish with a few crumbles of vegan feta

Directions:

1. Combine the quinoa and broth in a medium pot and bring to a boil over high heat.
2. Cover, reduce the heat to low, and cook until all the liquid has been absorbed, about 20 minutes. Remove from the heat and fluff with a fork. Allow to cool, uncovered, for 20 minutes.
3. Stir in the remaining ingredients and serve at room temperature. You can also store it in the refrigerator for at least an hour and serve it chilled.

TONI'S TIPS:

>>To shave down the cooking time, reduce the broth to 1½ cups and cook the quinoa in a pressure cooker for 5 minutes on high pressure with a quick release, then fluff the quinoa and continue with the recipe.

TESTERS' TIPS:

>>"This tastes great with a pinch of Dash seasoning."
—Shari T. from Valparaiso, IN

MY TIPS:

SPINACH ALFREDO

Serves 4 to 6 | Ready in 30 minutes

This decadent pasta dish was inspired by my dear friend and business partner, Michelle Cehn from WorldofVegan.com. She created a similar dish for our book, *The Friendly Vegan Cookbook,* and after making it a million times, I tailored it to fit my family's tastes. It's incredibly creamy thanks to cashews, and satisfies all of my comfort-food cravings, every time!

Ingredients:

1 cup raw cashews
7 cups vegetable or "No Chicken" broth, divided
1 tablespoon vegetable oil
1 small yellow onion, diced
5 garlic cloves, minced
1 (1-pound) package your favorite pasta
3 cups fresh spinach
Black pepper, to taste

Optional additions and swaps:

Swap the vegetable oil for ¼–½ cup water
Swap the vegetable oil for vegan butter
For more produce, add 1 cup sliced mushrooms in step 2
For more produce, add ⅔ cup frozen or canned peas in step 4
Swap the fresh spinach for 5 ounces frozen spinach
For spice, garnish with red chili flakes
Garnish with chopped fresh parsley
Add baked vegan breaded chicken nuggets when serving

Directions:

1. Using a high-powered blender, blend the cashews on the highest setting with 3 cups of the vegetable broth until a smooth and creamy milk forms, 3 to 4 minutes. (If you don't have a high-powered blender, soak the cashews in water overnight or boil them for 10 minutes, then drain and blend them in a standard blender. You'll need to blend for 5 to 6 minutes.)
2. In a large pot, heat the oil over medium heat. Add the onion and garlic and sauté until the onions become tender and translucent, 2 to 4 minutes.
3. Add the remaining 4 cups vegetable broth and the cashew milk mixture, increase the heat to medium-high, and bring to a boil.
4. Lower the heat to medium-low, add the pasta to the pot, and cook according to the package directions until tender. Stir the pasta frequently to prevent it from clumping and sticking to the bottom of the pot.

5. Turn off the heat, stir in the spinach, and allow the pasta and sauce to thicken on the stove for 5 minutes. If the sauce is still very liquidy, turn the heat back on while mixing the pasta and sauce for another 1 to 2 minutes—but keep in mind that the sauce will continue to thicken with time. Season with black pepper.

MY TIPS:

HUMMUS PASTA

Serves 4 | Ready in 20 minutes

By now, everybody has tried hummus as a bagel topping or dip for crackers and veggies, but have you ever tried it with pasta?! Switch up your pasta routine by using your favorite hummus as a sauce. You'll be amazed at how well the two go together, and you might even wish you had tried it sooner!

Ingredients:

1 (1-pound) package your favorite pasta
1 cup your favorite hummus
1 cup chopped sun-dried tomatoes
⅔ cup sliced kalamata olives
3 tablespoons minced fresh basil
2 tablespoons lemon juice

Optional additions and swaps:

Add ½ cup chopped fresh tomatoes in step 2
Swap the fresh basil for 2 teaspoons dried basil
For a more acidic taste, add an extra 1 tablespoon lemon juice

Directions:

1. In a large pot, cook the pasta according to the package instructions until tender. Drain, reserving ½ cup of the pasta water.
2. Return the cooked pasta and reserved pasta water to the same pot and stir in the remaining ingredients. Enjoy warm, at room temperature, or cold.

TONI'S TIPS:

>>Growing your own herbs—like basil, thyme, rosemary, and oregano—is really easy to do on a small piece of your yard, in a pot on a balcony, or in a planter on your windowsill. To dry them, simply cut a bunch, wash them, wrap the stems in a rubber band or ribbon, and hang them to dry in the sun (or even in your bedroom) for a few days. Then remove any tough stems and pulse the dried leaves in a food processor.

MY TIPS:

TOMATO BASIL QUINOA

Serves 4 | **Ready in 30 minutes**

One of my recipe testers said she loves how quickly this recipe comes together and believes everyone needs a go-to as simple and tasty as this in their cooking repertoire. I have to agree! Try it for a super satisfying lunch, or add the optional beans for a more substantial dinner.

Ingredients:

1 tablespoon olive oil
½ yellow or red onion, diced
3 garlic cloves, minced
1 cup diced tomatoes
1 cup quinoa
1¾ cups vegetable broth
½ cup chopped fresh basil

Optional additions and swaps:

Swap the oil for ¼ cup water
Stir in 1 (15-ounce) can garbanzo or white beans, drained and rinsed, in step 3
For spice, sprinkle on red chili flakes in step 3

Directions:

1. In a large pot, heat the oil over medium-high heat. Add the onion and sauté until tender and translucent, about 5 minutes.
2. Add the garlic and sauté for 1 minute. Add the tomatoes, quinoa, and broth and bring to a boil. Cover, lower the heat, and simmer until the liquid has been absorbed, about 20 minutes.
3. Fluff the quinoa and stir in the basil.

TONI'S TIPS:

>>If you're short on time, this dish can be made in a pressure cooker by reducing the broth to 1½ cups. Although it's not my preferred method because it doesn't have the exact texture of the stovetop version, it'll still taste great. Throw all the ingredients in the pot and cook on high pressure for 4 minutes with a quick release, then continue to step 3.

MY TIPS:

30-MINUTE MEALS

The key to a relaxed evening at home after a long day at work is a nourishing meal that doesn't require a lot of time to prepare. Each of these flavor-packed recipes has been designed to come together in just 30 minutes, and they're budget-friendly to boot. That means more time for doing the things you really enjoy with the people you love. What could be better than that?

PESTO PASTA

Serves 4 | Ready in 30 minutes

I love a recipe that allows you to work with ingredients you already have in your pantry, and this Pesto Pasta is just that. While typical pesto calls for expensive pine nuts, this version allows you to use more affordable and readily available pumpkin seeds, sunflower seeds, walnuts, or other nuts you have on hand.

Ingredients:

1 (1-pound) package your favorite pasta
1½ cups tightly packed fresh basil leaves
1 cup your choice raw nuts or seeds (walnuts, shelled sunflower or pumpkin seeds, etc.)
3 garlic cloves, peeled
½ cup olive oil
1 tablespoon lemon juice
1 teaspoon salt
Black pepper, to taste

Optional additions and swaps:

Swap the basil for parsley, spinach, arugula, or a combination of any of them
For spice, add a pinch of red chili flakes in step 2
Add 2 tablespoons nutritional yeast in step 2
Add 2 cups your favorite steamed veggies in step 3

Directions:

1. In a large pot, cook the pasta according to package instructions until tender. Drain and transfer to a large bowl.
2. Meanwhile, combine the basil, nuts or seeds, garlic, olive oil, lemon juice, and salt in a blender or food processor, and blend on high until smooth and creamy.
3. Stir the pesto in the pasta. Season with a few grinds of black pepper.

TONI'S TIPS:

>>Ice cube trays aren't just for making ice; try using one to preserve your pesto! Triple or quadruple the pesto in this recipe, pour it into an ice cube tray, freeze it, then pop out your pesto cubes and store them in an airtight container for up to 3 months. To reheat, in a medium pot, add 3 or 4 cubes (or more if you want extra flavor) to a serving of cooked pasta and heat over medium-high heat, stirring until they melt and become a sauce that evenly coats the pasta.

MY TIPS:

TOMATO BASIL ANGEL HAIR PASTA

Serves 4 to 6 | Ready in 25 minutes

In 2020, I developed an obsession with gardening. Hot Sacramento summers are perfect for growing tomatoes, and my backyard plants produced a bounty of cherry and Sungold varieties. This recipe was my go-to for transforming all those juicy tomatoes into quick, fresh, and incredibly delicious meals.

Ingredients:

1 (1-pound) package angel hair pasta
¼ cup olive oil
2 (1-pint) packages cherry or grape tomatoes, quartered
4 garlic cloves, minced
½ cup fresh basil leaves, chopped
½ teaspoon salt

Optional additions and swaps:

Swap the angel hair for your favorite pasta
If you're a garlic lover, double the garlic
For a cheesy taste, stir in 1 tablespoon nutritional yeast at the end of step 2
For an acidic taste, add a squeeze of lemon juice when serving
For spice, sprinkle on some red chili flakes when serving
Garnish with vegan parmesan cheese

Directions:

1. In a large pot, cook the pasta according to the package instructions until tender. Drain, reserving ½ cup of the pasta water.
2. In the same pot, heat the oil over medium heat. Add the tomatoes and garlic and cook for 2 or 3 minutes, gently mashing the tomatoes with the back of a spatula or wooden spoon.
3. Stir in the basil, salt, pasta, and reserved pasta water and let it sit for 1 to 2 minutes, until it begins to thicken.

TONI'S TIPS:

>>If you have bouillon paste or cubes, stir some into the pasta water to add depth of flavor to this dish.

MY TIPS:

UDON NOODLES WITH PEANUT SAUCE

Serves 4 to 6 | Ready in 15 minutes

I have a special love for Japanese noodles, and udon is one of my absolute favorites. I'm partial to cooking with the shelf-stable variety, but feel free to use the thicker noodles that come refrigerated. To make this a meal, serve it with Fried Tofu (page 142) and a side of steamed vegetables.

Ingredients:

1 (1-pound) package udon noodles

2 batches Peanut Sauce (page 180)

1 bunch green onions, sliced

¼ cup sesame seeds

Optional additions and swaps:

Swap the udon noodles for rice noodles, ramen noodles, or any Japanese-style noodles

For more texture, add ¼ cup chopped peanuts when serving

For a smoother sauce, add 1 tablespoon water to the peanut sauce before stirring it in

Directions:

1. In a large pot, cook the udon noodles according to the package instructions. Drain and transfer to a serving bowl.
2. Stir in the peanut sauce.
3. Top with the green onions and sesame seeds when serving.

TONI'S TIPS:

>>Level up your sesame seeds by toasting them in a small pan over medium-high heat for about 5 minutes, stirring frequently, or until lightly golden and fragrant.

If you have leftovers or are making this dish ahead, store in an airtight container in the refrigerator for up to 5 days. Serve cold or reheat in the microwave for 3 to 5 minutes.

MY TIPS:

SESAME GINGER NOODLES

Serves 4 to 6 | Ready in 25 minutes

This substantial noodle dish is a blank slate just waiting for you to engage your culinary creativity with whatever vegetables you have on hand. Grate some carrots, toss in some edamame, or add a handful of frozen broccoli florets to get the most out of this tasty meal.

Ingredients:

1 (1-pound) package udon noodles
1½ tablespoons toasted sesame oil
1 medium bell pepper (any color), thinly sliced
1 small red or yellow onion, thinly sliced
1½ tablespoons minced ginger
3 garlic cloves, minced
3 tablespoons soy sauce
1 bunch green onions, sliced
¼ cup sesame seeds

Optional additions and swaps:

Swap the udon noodles for rice noodles, ramen noodles, or any Japanese-style noodles
In a pinch you can swap the fresh ginger for ½ teaspoon ground ginger
For spice and more flavor, add ½–1 tablespoon sriracha in step 4
For protein, stir in 1 batch Fried Tofu (page 142) or 1 cup cooked edamame in step 4
For more nutrients, add 1–2 cups steamed vegetables in step 4
Offer extra soy sauce when serving

Directions:

1. In a large pot, cook the udon noodles according to the package instructions. Reserve 1 tablespoon of the pasta water, then drain the noodles.
2. While the udon noodles are boiling, in a large skillet, heat the oil over medium-high heat. Add the bell pepper and onion and sauté until the bell pepper is tender, 3 to 4 minutes.
3. Add the ginger and garlic and sauté until fragrant, about 1 minute.
4. Stir in the noodles, soy sauce, and reserved pasta water and cook for 1 to 2 minutes, until the flavors are melded together.
5. Top with the green onions and sesame seeds when serving.

MY TIPS:

TONI'S TIPS:

>> If you have leftovers or are making this dish ahead, store in an airtight container in the refrigerator for up to 5 days. Serve cold or reheat in the microwave for 3 to 5 minutes.

CAULIFLOWER FRIED RICE

Serves 2 to 4 | Ready in 25 minutes

I was a little late to the riced cauliflower trend, but since trying it, I've never looked back—it's tasty and packed with nutrients! To make this recipe even easier, look for pre-riced cauliflower at your local grocery store, where it can often be found in the frozen food section. You'll need about 2½ cups for this recipe.

Ingredients:

1 small head cauliflower, chopped
1 tablespoon toasted sesame oil
1 (10-ounce) bag frozen mixed vegetables
½ medium yellow or red onion, diced
2 large garlic cloves, minced
½ (14- to 16-ounce) package extra- or super-firm tofu, drained and pressed
3 tablespoons soy sauce

Optional additions and swaps:

Swap the oil for ¼–½ cup vegetable broth
Swap cauliflower for 2½ cups cooked white or brown rice
For extra flavor, add 1½ teaspoons minced ginger in step 2
Serve with a dash of sriracha
Garnish with sliced green onions

Directions:

1. In a food processor, pulse the cauliflower 15 to 20 times, until it begins to look like rice. Set aside.
2. In a large skillet, heat the oil over medium-high heat. Add the frozen vegetables, onion, and garlic and cook until the onion is tender and translucent, about 5 minutes.
3. Using your fingers, crumble the tofu into the skillet and cook until the tofu begins to turn golden, about 5 minutes.
4. Add the riced cauliflower and soy sauce and sauté, stirring frequently, until the cauliflower is tender, 5 to 8 minutes.

MY TIPS:

ASPARAGUS AND RICE STIR-FRY

Serves 4 | Ready in 20 minutes

Growing up in a home with a Japanese grandfather meant we always had steamed rice on hand. Before leftover rice became too hard in the fridge, my grandma would prepare a quick stir-fry with some vegetables and soy sauce. This dish is an homage to them both and never fails to conjure up fond memories of my childhood.

Ingredients:

1½ tablespoons olive or vegetable oil
½ (14- to 16-ounce) package extra- or super-firm tofu, pressed and cut into ½-inch cubes
2 cups chopped asparagus (1-inch pieces)
1 small yellow or red onion, diced
2 tablespoons garlic chili sauce
2 tablespoons soy sauce
3 cups cooked brown or white rice
1 bunch green onions, sliced

Optional additions and swaps:

For more flavor, swap 1½ teaspoons of the olive or vegetable oil for toasted sesame oil
Omit the rice, use the whole package of tofu, and add 1 cup frozen veggies in step 1
Swap the asparagus for 2 cups frozen mixed vegetables
Swap the garlic chili sauce for 3 minced garlic cloves + 1½ tablespoon sriracha
For more flavor, add 1½ teaspoons minced ginger in step 1

Directions:

1. In a large skillet or wok, heat the oil over medium-high heat. Add the tofu and asparagus and sauté, stirring occasionally, until the tofu is golden on all sides, about 5 minutes.
2. Stir in the onion, garlic chili sauce, and soy sauce and sauté until the onion is tender, 3 to 4 minutes. If the onion is cooking too quickly, reduce the heat to medium.
3. Stir in the rice and sauté until heated through, 1 to 2 minutes. Top with the green onions when serving.

TONI'S TIPS:

>>For those of you who are new to garlic chili sauce, this can be found in the Asian foods section of most grocery stores. It packs some spice!

MY TIPS:

LEMON BASIL TOFU

Serves 4 | Ready in 25 minutes

Citrus and basil is a classic flavor combination, and those flavors shine bright in this scrumptious tofu dish. Pair it with some brown rice for a savory feast that will make your tastebuds dance.

Ingredients:

¼ cup soy sauce
3½ tablespoons lemon juice
1½ teaspoons agave or maple syrup
1 tablespoon vegetable oil
½ large yellow or red onion, sliced
1 small green or red bell pepper, sliced
4 garlic cloves, minced
1 tablespoon minced ginger
1 (14- to 16-ounce) package extra- or super-firm tofu, drained, pressed, and cut into 1-inch cubes
¼ cup packed fresh basil leaves, chopped

Optional additions and swaps:

If you don't have fresh ginger, ½ teaspoon ground ginger will work
For spice, add a pinch of red chili flakes or a squirt of sriracha in step 2
For more acidity, add ½–1 teaspoon extra agave in step 2
If the sauce is too sweet for you, add another ½–1 tablespoon lemon juice
Swap the vegetable oil for toasted sesame oil or ¼ cup vegetable broth
For more color, add ¾ cup snap peas in step 3
Serve over steamed brown rice
Garnish with sesame seeds

Directions:

1. In a small bowl, whisk together the soy sauce, lemon juice, and agave or maple syrup. Set aside.
2. In a large skillet, heat the oil over medium-high heat. Add the onion and bell pepper and sauté until the veggies begin to become tender, 1 to 2 minutes. Stir in the garlic and ginger and sauté until the bell pepper is tender, 1 to 2 minutes.
3. Scoot the veggies out of the way with a spatula and add the tofu cubes to the center of the pan. Cook the tofu cubes for 1 minute on each side.
4. Pour in the soy sauce mixture and add the basil. Cook for 3 minutes, then flip the tofu cubes over and cook until lightly browned and warmed all the way through, about 3 more minutes.

TESTERS' TIPS:

>>"For a deeper flavor in the tofu, marinate it in the sauce for a few hours, or better yet, overnight." —Brooks P. from Sacramento, CA

MY TIPS:

SOUTHWESTERN LETTUCE WRAPS

Serves 2 to 4 | Ready in 30 minutes

Lettuce wraps are most often inspired by East Asian flavors, but I've discovered they lend themselves really well to the earthy flavors of the American Southwest. This recipe brims with color and texture—plus it's easy to make, and even easier to eat!

Ingredients:

1½ tablespoons vegetable oil
1 small red or green bell pepper, diced
1 small red onion, diced
1 (15-ounce) can corn kernels, drained and rinsed
3 garlic cloves, minced
1 (15-ounce) can black beans, drained and rinsed
¼ cup packed minced fresh cilantro
1 teaspoon chili powder
Salt, to taste
Juice of ½–1 lemon
Large lettuce leaves (romaine, butter lettuce, iceberg, etc.)

Optional additions and swaps:

Swap the oil for vegan butter
Swap the oil for ½ cup water or vegetable broth
Garnish with avocado slices
Garnish with diced tomatoes
Add a dash of hot sauce when serving
Top with Cashew Crema (page 190) when serving

Directions:

1. In a large skillet, heat the oil over medium-high heat. Add the bell pepper and onion and sauté until the veggies start to become tender, 1 to 2 minutes.
2. Add the corn and garlic and sauté for 5 minutes.
3. Stir in the beans, cilantro, chili powder, salt, and lemon juice (start with ½ of the lemon and add more at the end if you'd like more tang) and cook just until heated through.
4. Allow to cool for 5 minutes, then serve in lettuce leaves.

TESTERS' TIPS:

>>"Fry up some tofu to give it even more substance when you're feeding the whole family."
—Jami G. from La Crosse, WI

MY TIPS:

POTATO TACOS

Serves 4 to 6 | Ready in 30 minutes

I've been loving Potato Tacos—also known as Tacos de Papas—since long before my vegan days. Back then, they were my go-to whenever I dined at Mexican restaurants, and I still love them all these years later. To take these tacos to the next level, fry your tortillas before stuffing with the potato mixture. (See instructions in my tip below.) So good!

Ingredients:

2 large russet potatoes, scrubbed and cut into 1-inch pieces
3 tablespoons vegan butter
1 small red or yellow onion, finely diced
3 garlic cloves, minced
¾ teaspoon seasoned salt
10 corn tortillas
1 cup shredded iceberg lettuce
2 Roma tomatoes, diced

Optional additions and swaps:

Swap the vegan butter for ¼ cup vegetable broth
Garnish with diced avocado
Use store-bought or homemade crispy taco shells

Directions:

1. Put the potatoes in a large pot and cover with water. Bring to a boil and cook for 7 to 9 minutes, or until the potatoes are tender. Drain the potatoes and set aside.
2. In the same pot, melt the vegan butter over medium-high heat. Add the onion and garlic and sauté until the onion is tender and translucent, 3 to 4 minutes.
3. Add the potatoes and seasoned salt and lightly mash the potatoes with the back of a wooden spoon or strong spatula. Remove from the heat.
4. Warm each tortillas in a large skillet over high heat for about 45 seconds, then flip.
5. Scoop a spoonful of the potato mixture onto each tortilla and garnish with lettuce and tomatoes. Any leftover potato mixture can be stored in an airtight container in the refrigerator for up to 5 days.

TONI'S TIPS:

>>Making your own fried tortilla shells is the secret to off-the-charts tasty tacos, like the ones shown in the photo. Start by heating about 2 tablespoons high-heat oil (like canola) in a small skillet over high heat. When the oil is hot, use tongs to add a tortilla and let it cook for about 10 seconds, flip it over (again, with tongs), and then use

the tongs to gently fold the tortilla in half. Allow the folded tortilla to cook for 5 seconds on each side, or just until they begin to turn golden. For something a little extra, you can sprinkle the outside of the shells with vegan parmesan. To keep them warm while making a big batch, place them on a baking sheet in the oven preheated to 200 degrees.

MY TIPS:

HUMMUS PIZZA

Serves 6 to 8 | Ready in 20 minutes

For those times when I can't bear the thought of tackling a pile of dishes, this Hummus Pizza saves the day. Just pop a crust into the oven and bake until golden, top with hummus and fresh vegetables, and devour. You'll find so much flavor and texture in every bite!

Ingredients:

1 store-bought or homemade pizza crust
1 cup hummus
⅓ cup diced cucumbers
⅓ cup diced tomatoes
⅓ cup kalamata olives
⅓ cup packed baby spinach

Optional additions and swaps:

Add ¼ cup finely diced red onion in step 2
For more protein, slice up vegan lunch meat and add it in step 2
Swap the kalamata olives for black olives
For more heartiness, add ⅓ cup chopped marinated artichoke hearts
For spice, add 1 sliced jalapeño or serrano pepper
For spice, add 1 teaspoon red chili flakes

Directions:

1. Prepare the pizza crust according to the package or recipe instructions.
2. Spread the hummus evenly over the baked crust. Top with the cucumbers, tomatoes, olives, and spinach.
3. Slice the pizza and serve right away.

TESTERS' TIPS:

>>"This is also great baked with extra vegetables at 375 degrees for 8 to 12 minutes." —Jill S. from Tiffin, IA

MY TIPS:

STUFFED SWEET POTATOES (3 WAYS)

Serves 4 to 6 | Ready in 10 minutes

I'm such a huge fan of stuffed sweet potatoes that I put a pair of them on the cover of my *Plant-Based on a Budget* cookbook! They're not just eye-catchingly colorful, but nutritious, tasty, and infinitely versatile. Those were stuffed with beans, corn, and tomatoes—still one of my favorite combos—but that recipe is just a jumping-off point for a variety of dishes with different flavors. Try these three options, stuffing your sweet pots with my Calabacitas (zucchini, corn, and tomatoes), Tabbouleh-Inspired Quinoa, and/or Simple Black Bean Chili, and you'll become an instant fan, too.

Ingredients:

4 sweet potatoes, well scrubbed
1 batch Calabacitas (page 158), Tabbouleh-Inspired Quinoa (page 82), or Simple Black Bean Chili (page 68)

Optional additions:

Calabacitas-stuffed potatoes are great topped with cooked lentils (page 152, or the Lentil Taco stuffing from the Plant-Based on a Budget cookbook) plus a dollop of Cashew Crema (page 190) or store-bought vegan sour cream
Quinoa-stuffed potatoes are excellent topped with vegan feta cheese and cooked or canned garbanzo beans
Chili-stuffed potatoes are delicious topped with a dollop of Cashew Crema (page 190), a squeeze of lime juice, and some minced fresh cilantro

Directions:

1. With a fork, poke holes all over the sweet potatoes for ventilation.
2. Put the potatoes on a microwave-safe plate and microwave for 2 minutes, then flip and microwave for another 2 minutes, or until the potatoes are soft and cooked through. If they need more time, microwave again in 1-minute increments until soft, checking for doneness and flipping after each additional minute.
3. Cut the sweet potatoes in half lengthwise. Using a spoon, mash the insides of the sweet potatoes, leaving the flesh inside the skins.
4. Top the sweet potatoes with your choice of filling and any additional add-ons you like.

MY TIPS:

TONI'S TIPS:

>>Don't have a microwave? Try steaming your sweet potatoes in a steamer basket for 25 minutes or baking them at 425 degrees for 50 minutes or until fork-tender.

SHEET PAN DISHES AND CASSEROLES

When it's cold outside, I love to warm up my home with the savory aromas from my favorite sheet pan dishes and comforting casseroles. These meals have the added advantage of keeping dirty dishes to a minimum and making great leftovers that last throughout the week.

TATER TOT CASSEROLE

Serves 4 to 6 | Ready in 45 minutes

Tater tots are great stand-ins for hash browns, making this casserole a hearty breakfast option for cold winter mornings, but I'm known to make it for dinner, too! It's hearty, packed with protein, and deliciously satiating.

Ingredients:

1 tablespoon vegetable oil
½ bell pepper (any color), diced
½ medium onion, diced
3 garlic cloves, minced
1 (14- to 16-ounce) package extra- or super-firm tofu, drained and pressed
½ teaspoon ground turmeric
½ teaspoon salt
½ teaspoon black pepper
1 (19-ounce) package frozen tater tots

Optional additions and swaps:

Swap the oil for ½ cup vegetable broth or water
Swap the fresh bell pepper for 1 cup sliced frozen bell pepper
To make it creamier and eggy, add 1½ tablespoons vegan butter in step 3
Make it heartier by adding sliced vegan breakfast sausage in step 2
Sprinkle vegan cheese on the tofu mixture in step 4 before adding the tater tots

Directions:

1. Preheat the oven to the temperature directed on your tater tots package.
2. In a large skillet, heat the oil over medium heat. Add the bell pepper, onion, and garlic and sauté, stirring occasionally, until the bell pepper and onion are tender, 5 to 7 minutes.
3. Using your fingers, crumble the tofu into the skillet. Add the turmeric, salt, and pepper and mix thoroughly. Cook until the flavors are melded together, 3 to 5 minutes.
4. Transfer the tofu mixture to an 8-inch square baking pan and cover the top with the frozen tater tots.
5. Bake for the time directed on the tater tot package (usually 20 to 25 minutes). If they are not golden brown, you can bake a little longer, checking in 5-minute increments, until they reach your desired crispness.

TONI'S TIPS:

>>To make this casserole ahead and freeze it, follow steps 2 and 3 and allow the tofu mixture to cool completely. Continue with step 4, making sure to use a freezer-to-oven-friendly pan, then cover the pan tightly with aluminum foil and store in the freezer for up to 1 month. When you're ready to eat, preheat the oven and bake as instructed in step 5.

MY TIPS:

CHILI CORNBREAD CASSEROLE

Serves 6 to 8 | Ready in 45 minutes (30 minutes to cook, 15 minutes to cool)

You might recognize this seriously delicious cornbread recipe that I developed from *The Friendly Vegan Cookbook*. It was such a hit that I had to bring it back—with a twist—for this filling Cornbread Casserole. Serve it with a fresh salad for a nourishing weeknight dinner.

Ingredients:

2 tablespoons flaxseed meal
5 tablespoons warm water
1 cup all-purpose flour
1 cup cornmeal
½ cup granulated sugar
1 tablespoon + 1 teaspoon baking powder
1 teaspoon salt
¼ cup vegetable oil
1 cup plant-based milk
1 batch Simple Black Bean Chili (page 68)

Optional addition:

Add ¾ cup fresh, frozen, or canned corn kernels to the cornbread batter in step 4

Directions:

1. Preheat the oven to 425 degrees.
2. In a small bowl, whisk together the flaxseed meal and warm water for 1 minute. Set aside for 5 minutes to thicken.
3. In a large bowl, combine the flour, cornmeal, sugar, baking powder, and salt.
4. Pour in the oil, plant-based milk, and flaxseed mixture and mix by hand until combined.
5. Pour the chili into a 9 × 13-inch casserole dish and spread it into an even layer.
6. Using a spoon, dollop the cornbread batter onto the chili. It's okay if it doesn't completely cover the chili.
7. Bake for 20 minutes.
8. Allow to cool for 15 minutes before serving.

TONI'S TIPS:

>>You can also make the cornbread as a stand-alone recipe by pouring the batter into an 8-inch baking pan or cast-iron skillet and baking for 20 minutes at 425 degrees.

MY TIPS:

PASTA BAKE

Serves 6 to 8 | Ready in 35 minutes

In this savory pasta bake, tofu stands in for ricotta, lending a delicate texture, a boost of protein, and a hint of oregano for a classic Italian taste.

Ingredients:

1 (1-pound) package your favorite pasta
1 tablespoon vegetable oil
1 small yellow or red onion, diced
3 garlic cloves, minced
2 teaspoons dried oregano
1 (14- to 16-ounce) package extra- or super-firm tofu, drained and pressed
¼ teaspoon salt
2 cups packed chopped spinach
1 (25-ounce) jar marinara sauce

Optional additions and swaps:

Swap the oil for ¼ cup water or vegetable broth
Add 1 cup frozen broccoli florets or mushrooms in step 3
Add ¼ cup frozen peas in step 3
For a cheesier taste, add ½–1 tablespoon nutritional yeast in step 4

Directions:

1. Preheat the oven to 350 degrees.
2. In a large pot, cook the pasta according to the package instructions until tender.
3. While the pasta cooks, in a large skillet, heat the oil over medium-high heat. Add the onion, garlic, and oregano and sauté until the onion is tender and translucent, 2 to 3 minutes.
4. Using your fingers, crumble the tofu into the skillet and cook for another 5 minutes. Stir in the salt and spinach.
5. While the tofu cooks, check on the pasta. When it's done, drain the pasta and return it to the pot. Pour in the marinara and stir until evenly coated.
6. Pour the pasta and sauce into a 9 × 13-inch casserole dish and spread into an even layer. Using a spoon, dollop the tofu mixture evenly onto the pasta.
7. Bake for 10 minutes, until it's cooked all the way through and slightly toasted on top.

MY TIPS:

SHEET PAN FAJITAS

Serves 4 | **Ready in 35 minutes**

When you've got a pan of these fajitas baking in the oven, your home will fill up with some of my all-time favorite aromas. This mix of peppers, onions, and tofu doesn't just smell amazing, though—it's also extremely tasty! Besides fajitas, try it stuffed inside tacos and burritos.

Ingredients:

½ (14- to 16-ounce) package extra- or super-firm tofu, drained and pressed
2 bell peppers (any color), sliced
1 red or yellow onion, sliced
3 garlic cloves, minced
2 tablespoons taco seasoning (store-bought or see Toni's Tips below)
2 tablespoons vegetable oil

Optional additions and swaps:

Swap the fresh bell peppers for a 14-ounce bag frozen bell peppers (no need to thaw)
Add 1 cup sliced mushrooms in step 3
For a subtle cheesy taste, add 1½ teaspoons nutritional yeast in step 3
For more flavor, add 1½ teaspoons more taco seasoning in step 3
Serve with warm tortillas
Garnish with minced fresh cilantro
Garnish with diced avocado
Garnish with shredded vegan cheese or sour cream
Serve with lime wedges for squeezing
Serve with salsa

Directions:

1. Preheat the oven to 425 degrees. Line a rimmed baking sheet with a silicone mat or parchment paper.
2. Using your fingers, pull the tofu into 1-inch chunks and scatter them on the prepared sheet pan.
3. Add the bell peppers, onion, garlic, taco seasoning, and oil. Stir until everything is evenly coated, then spread it all out in a single layer.
4. Bake for 25 minutes. (If you're using frozen bell peppers, add 5 more minutes.)

TONI'S TIPS:

>>To save time, I recommend using store-bought taco seasoning, but you can make your own simple seasoning with the following recipe. In a small jar, combine 2½ teaspoons chili powder, 2½ teaspoons ground cumin, 1½ teaspoons smoked paprika, and

½–¾ teaspoon salt. Store in a cool, dry place until you're ready to use it. It's not just for Mexican food—try sprinkling it over popcorn on your next movie night for a twist on the classic cinema snack.

TESTERS' TIPS:

>>"If you want to switch things up, you can also put the fajita filling into a hummus wrap." —Micah J. from Germany

MY TIPS:

SHEET PAN PIZZA

Makes 1 pizza; serves 2 to 4 | Ready in 30 minutes

Sheet pan pizzas are so customizable! My husband prefers his made with a whole wheat crust, nutritional yeast, and all the mushrooms his heart desires, and I love mine with vegan cheese, oodles of veggies, and vegan chicken nuggets.

There are plenty of pre-made vegan pizza doughs out there. Pillsbury makes one (look for the blue tube), and Trader Joe's has three flavors: plain, whole wheat, and spinach. My absolute favorite, however, is the homemade option called Lora's Pizza Dough in the *Plant-Based on a Budget* cookbook. Whichever you choose, I bet you'll be pleasantly surprised by how easy it is to make your own pizza—and it'll probably be ready even faster than delivery could reach your door!

Ingredients:

1 (13- to 16-ounce) package refrigerated or thawed frozen pizza dough
1 cup pizza sauce or thick marinara sauce
1½ cups your favorite sliced toppings (zucchini, mushrooms, onion, garlic, olives, bell pepper, etc.)

Optional additions and swaps:

Swap the pizza sauce for BBQ sauce
Add vegan cheese in step 3 after spreading the sauce
Add vegan pepperoni slices in step 3
Add prebaked vegan chicken nuggets in step 3

Directions:

1. Preheat the oven according to your pizza dough instructions. Line a rimmed baking sheet with a silicone mat or parchment paper.
2. If your dough requires rolling, roll it out using a rolling pin on a lightly floured surface to fit your prepared baking sheet. It's sometimes easier to do this directly on the baking sheet covered with a silicone mat or parchment paper so you don't have to transfer it. You can also stretch it in the pan using your fingers. If your dough requires prebaking, do so.
3. Evenly spread the pizza sauce over the dough. Scatter your vegetables evenly on top of the sauce.
4. Bake according to your crust instructions.

TONI'S TIPS:

>>You can store leftover pizza in an airtight container in the refrigerator for up to 5 days or in the freezer for up to 3 months. To reheat, preheat the oven to 350 degrees and bake for 5 minutes if refrigerated or 8 to 10 minutes if frozen.

MY TIPS:

MINI PIZZA BAGELS

Makes 10 bagel pizzas | Ready in 25 minutes

My dad is the source of so many wonderful food memories. When I was young, he would keep the freezer stocked with Bagel Bites. Now, I make them at home, and in just one bite, I'm instantly transported back to childhood! Level them up by adding vegan cheese.

Ingredients:

5 mini bagels
1½ cups pizza sauce or thick marinara sauce
½ cup finely chopped veggies (mushrooms, bell pepper, onion, olives, zucchini, etc.)

Optional additions and swaps:

Swap the mini bagels for English muffins
Sprinkle 1½ cups shredded vegan cheese on top of the sauce in step 2
Garnish with 2 tablespoons minced fresh basil

MY TIPS:

Directions:

1. Preheat the oven to 375 degrees. If you like, line a rimmed baking sheet with parchment paper or a silicone mat. (This isn't totally necessary since the prebaked bagels aren't likely to stick to the sheet, but if you're worried about the sauce or veggies spilling over, go for it.)
2. If your bagels aren't already cut, slice them in half. Lay the bagel halves cut-side up on the baking sheet. Spoon some sauce on each bagel and scatter the veggies on top.
3. Bake for 10 to 12 minutes, or until the bagels are crispy and the veggies are tender. If you're using vegan cheese and want it to be melted, broil for 1 to 2 minutes, watching closely so it doesn't burn.

TONI'S TIPS:

>>These freeze beautifully. After step 2, place the baking sheet (lined with a silicone mat or parchment paper) in the freezer for 1 to 2 hours, until the bagel pizzas are completely frozen, then transfer to an airtight container and store for up to 2 months. When ready to eat, preheat the oven to 375 degrees and continue to step 3.

TESTERS' TIPS:

>>"These work great in an air fryer by preheating it to 375 degrees and cooking for 6 minutes. If using vegan cheese, cook for 1 minute before adding additional toppings."
—Amber L. from Peoria, AZ

SHEET PAN RATATOUILLE

Serves 6 | Ready in 1 hour 15 minutes

This recipe does take a while from start to finish, but because the ratatouille is in the oven for the majority of that time, I still consider this a quick and easy dish! Unlike some ratatouille recipes that have you layer thinly sliced vegetables in an ornate spiral design, here the veggies are simply diced and tossed together on a sheet pan—no need to worry about your design or stand stirring a pot on the stove. There's so much to love about ratatouille, especially its versatility. Try it atop rice, a hollowed out roasted squash, or pasta, or spoon it over a thick slice of bread and top with your favorite vegan cheese, then grill under a broiler until the cheese is bubbly for a heavenly open-faced sandwich.

Ingredients:

1 medium eggplant, diced
1 medium zucchini, diced
1 medium yellow summer squash, diced
3 large Roma tomatoes, diced
½ yellow or red onion, diced
½ green or red bell pepper, diced
8 garlic cloves, sliced
¼ cup olive oil
2 tablespoons balsamic vinegar
1 teaspoon salt
½ cup fresh basil, chopped

Optional addition:

For protein, add 1 cup cooked or canned white beans in step 4

Directions:

1. Preheat the oven to 375 degrees. Line a rimmed baking sheet with a silicone mat or parchment paper.
2. Combine all the vegetables on the prepared baking sheet and add the oil, vinegar, and salt. Stir together until thoroughly mixed, then spread everything out into an even layer. Bake for 30 minutes.
3. Remove from the oven, toss the veggies, and bake for another 25 minutes, or until the veggies are tender.
4. Remove from the oven, stir in the basil, and bake for 5 more minutes.

MY TIPS:

VEGETABLE AND GARBANZO BEAN FOIL PACKETS

Serves 5 | Ready in 40 minutes

These handy packets stuffed with a medley of veggies and beans offer plenty of mealtime possibilities. Heat and eat with your favorite grain, stir them into stews, or spoon over a baked potato. The options are endless!

Ingredients:

2 heads garlic, broken up and peeled
2 large red or yellow onions, sliced
2 large broccoli crowns, cut into bite-size florets
2 red or green bell peppers, sliced
4 carrots, sliced
1 (15-ounce) can garbanzo beans, drained and rinsed
¾ cup your favorite salad dressing
1 teaspoon garlic salt
Black pepper, to taste

Optional additions and swaps:

Swap in your favorite chopped frozen or fresh vegetables
For more flavor, add ½ teaspoon onion powder in step 2
For more flavor, add ½ teaspoon garlic powder in step 2

Directions:

1. If you're planning to serve these right away, preheat the oven to 400 degrees.
2. In a large bowl, mix together all the ingredients until thoroughly combined.
3. Lay out 5 pieces of aluminum foil, about 14 × 10 inches each. Divide the vegetable mix between the foil sheets. Tightly seal into packets by folding one side of the foil over the other and crimping/folding the edges.
4. If you're making these ahead, transfer the packets to the fridge for up to 1 week or to the freezer for up to 2 months. When you're ready to eat, preheat the oven to 400 degrees, place the packets on a rimmed baking sheet, and bake for 25 minutes.

TONI'S TIP:

>>These also come out great in a toaster oven!

MY TIPS:

SHEET PAN NACHOS

Serves 4 to 6 | Ready in 20 minutes

These Sheet Pan Nachos come together quickly for a filling lunch, festive appetizer, or even a main course at dinner. If you're skipping the store-bought vegan cheese, try the Nacho Sauce from the *Plant-Based on a Budget* cookbook instead for an old-school nachos experience—just drizzle it on after baking.

Ingredients:

1 (14.5-ounce) can diced tomatoes, drained
1 (15-ounce) can black beans, drained and rinsed
1 (15.25-ounce) can corn kernels, drained
1½ tablespoons taco seasoning (store-bought or page 122)
1 (12-ounce) bag tortilla chips
⅓ cup jarred sliced nacho jalapeños, drained

Optional additions:

Add 2 cups shredded vegan cheese in step 3 after laying down the tortilla chips
Add vegan meat crumbles in step 3
Garnish with a handful of minced fresh cilantro
Garnish with avocado slices or a dollop or two of guacamole
Garnish with a dollop of store-bought vegan sour cream or a drizzle of Cashew Crema page 190)

Directions:

1. Preheat the oven to 400 degrees.
2. With a clean kitchen towel or several paper towels, blot the tomatoes, beans, and corn to remove excess moisture. Combine them in a large bowl and stir in the taco seasoning.
3. Spread out the tortilla chips on a rimmed baking sheet. Evenly top with the bean mixture and sliced nacho jalapeños.
4. Bake for 8 minutes. Serve immediately.

TONI'S TIPS:

>>Removing excess moisture is very important to avoid soggy nachos.

MY TIPS:

CHICK'N AND RICE CASSEROLE

Serves 4 | Ready in 50 minutes

This recipe falls into the classic casserole category, and just like those yummy one-pot dishes of yore, this one stands the test of time, tasting even better the next day. Most of the prep time is inactive—the casserole bakes for 40 minutes, freeing you up to get other things done while dinner comes together. To give the casserole a cheesy flavor, sprinkle a little nutritional yeast or vegan parmesan on top before serving.

Ingredients:

2¼ cups vegetable or "No Chicken" broth
1 cup long-grain white rice
1 teaspoon garlic powder
1 teaspoon onion powder
½ teaspoon salt
1 (1-pound) bag frozen mixed vegetables
1 (14- to 16-ounce) package extra- or super-firm tofu, drained and pressed
Salt and black pepper, to taste

Optional additions and swaps:

For more flavor, stir in 2 tablespoons minced fresh parsley after baking
Swap the frozen veggies for a (15-ounce) can mixed veggies, drained

Directions:

1. Preheat the oven to 400 degrees.
2. In a small pot, bring the broth to a boil. (Alternatively, you can microwave it for 2 minutes in a microwave-safe dish.)
3. In a 9 × 13-inch casserole dish, evenly spread out the rice and add an even layer of vegetables on top.
4. Pour the hot broth on top of the rice and vegetables.
5. Using your fingers, pull apart the tofu into 1-inch chunks and scatter them on top of the vegetable-rice mixture.
6. Tightly cover the casserole dish with aluminum foil and bake on the center rack for 40 minutes. Season with salt and pepper.

MY TIPS:

SCALLOPED POTATOES

Serves 8 | Ready in 1½ hours

Due to its long baking time, I went back and forth trying to decide whether or not to include this recipe in this book. But because it's the most popular recipe on PlantBasedonaBudget.com, and because this book's photographer, Alfonso, says cheesy potatoes are eaten as a main course in his home country of Peru, I decided to include it. Enjoy it on an evening when you're a little less crunched for time!

Ingredients:

- 4 pounds russet potatoes
- ¼ cup + 2 tablespoons vegan butter
- ¼ cup + 2 tablespoons all-purpose flour
- 3 cups plant-based milk
- 1½ cups vegetable broth
- ½ cup nutritional yeast
- 2 teaspoons garlic powder
- 2 teaspoons onion powder
- 1½ teaspoons salt

MY TIPS:

Directions:

1. Preheat the oven to 400 degrees.
2. Thinly slice the potatoes into ⅛-inch rounds. I like to keep the peels on for nutrition and time-saving reasons, but you're welcome to peel them first. If you have a mandoline or food processor slicer attachment, that'll save time. If you're cutting by hand, do your best to cut them all uniformly or the baking time will be off.
3. In a large pot, melt the vegan butter over medium heat. Whisk in the flour and stir until the sauce thickens and becomes a roux, 3 to 5 minutes.
4. Whisk the plant-based milk and vegetable broth into the roux. Stir in the nutritional yeast, garlic powder, onion powder, and salt until the sauce thickens, 5 to 8 minutes.
5. Ladle a spoonful of cheesy sauce in a 9 × 13-inch casserole dish.
6. Layer one-fourth of the potatoes in the casserole dish, then pour one-fourth of the sauce on top, spreading evenly over the potatoes and allowing it to seep through the cracks. Continue the process three more times, ending with the remaining sauce on top. Tightly cover the casserole dish with aluminum foil and bake for 30 minutes.
7. Uncover the dish and bake for another 30 minutes.

TESTERS' TIPS:

>>"My mom always added thinly sliced onion when cooking her scalloped potatoes, and I highly recommend it!" —Kristen A. from Dayville, CT

MIX-AND-MATCH BOWLS

Of all the recipes in this book, it's the ones featured in this chapter that most accurately reflect the way my husband and I eat on a regular basis. For instance, I'll cook a big batch of quinoa for the week, and then, for a weeknight dinner, I'll make a quick and healthy meal by pairing the quinoa with cooked tofu or beans, a tasty sauce, and cooked veggies. Many evenings, I'll even take shortcuts by throwing together our premade grains with a can of drained and rinsed garbanzo beans, a store-bought sauce, and some veggies. Having a variety of canned beans and frozen vegetables on hand means the sky's the limit for your mix-and-match bowls!

Proteins

Vegetables

Basic Grains and Bases

Condiments

GINGER LIME TEMPEH

Serves 2 to 4 | Ready in 20 minutes

On its own, tempeh has a neutral, somewhat nutty flavor, which lends it to a variety of marinades and seasoning possibilities. I love the tempeh bacon in the first *Plant-Based on a Budget* cookbook, but this flavorful recipe is my absolute favorite. If, however, you're not a fan of ginger, simply omit it.

Ingredients:

1 tablespoon vegetable oil
1 small yellow or red onion, diced
3 garlic cloves, minced
1½ teaspoons minced ginger
1 (8-ounce) package tempeh
2 tablespoons soy sauce
1½ tablespoons lime juice
1 teaspoon agave or maple syrup

Optional additions:

Add a small diced bell pepper (any color) in step 1
Garnish with minced fresh cilantro
Serve with lime wedges for squeezing
For spice, add a bit of red chili flakes or hot sauce when serving

Directions:

1. In a large skillet, heat the oil over medium-high heat. Add the onion, garlic, and ginger and sauté until fragrant, about 1 minute. Using your fingers, crumble the tempeh directly into the skillet and sauté, stirring frequently, until the tempeh is lightly browned, 1 to 2 minutes.
2. Pour in the soy sauce, lime juice, and your choice of a liquid sweetener and stir until the liquid is absorbed and the tempeh is slightly caramelized, about 5 minutes.
3. Serve right away, or store the tempeh in an airtight container in the fridge for up to 5 days. To reheat, warm gently in a skillet on the stovetop, or microwave in a microwave-safe bowl in 30-second increments until hot.

TONI'S TIPS:

>>To freeze, allow the tempeh to cool completely. Store in an airtight container in the freezer for up to 2 months. To thaw, refrigerate overnight or microwave in a microwave-safe bowl in 30-second increments.

TESTERS' TIPS:

>>"This would be great as taco 'meat,' on a pizza, as a breakfast with toast and avocado, and more."
—Heather W-C. from Denison, TX

MY TIPS:

FRIED TOFU

Before I learned how to prepare tofu, I hated it. My grandpa would prepare it by making slits on the top of a raw tofu block, pouring a little soy sauce on top, and then eating it just like that. Not my jam! Now, though, I love it. Freezing the tofu before cooking it changes its texture, making it firmer and chewier, but you can skip it to save time; simply drain and press the tofu as usual, then continue with step 4. You can also swap out the soy sauce and pepper for your favorite marinade. This is a recipe I like to triple or quadruple.

STOVETOP METHOD

Serves 2 | Ready in 50 minutes (plus freezing time)

Ingredients:

1 (14- to 16-ounce) package super- or extra-firm tofu
2 tablespoons soy sauce
¼ teaspoon black pepper, or to taste
1½ tablespoons vegetable oil or toasted sesame oil

Directions:

1. Place the unopened package of tofu in the freezer for at least 4 hours, or as long as 3 months.
2. Bring a pot of water to a boil. Remove the frozen tofu from its package and add it to the pot. Boil the tofu for 10 minutes.
3. Remove the tofu from the pot and let cool. When cool enough to handle, gently press the water out of the tofu with a clean kitchen towel. Be careful not to break the tofu.
4. Cut the tofu into ½-inch cubes and place in a medium bowl. Add the soy sauce and pepper and mix together. Let the tofu marinate for 30 minutes (or longer) in the refrigerator.
5. In a large skillet, heat the oil over high heat. Add the tofu cubes and fry until they turn golden all over, 1 to 2 minutes on each side. Transfer the tofu to a plate lined with a kitchen towel or paper towel to soak up the excess oil.
6. Serve right away, or store in an airtight container in the fridge for up to 5 days. To reheat, warm gently in a skillet on the stovetop, or microwave in a microwave-safe bowl in 30-second increments until hot.

AIR FRYER METHOD

Serves 2 | Ready in 1 hour (plus freezing time)

Ingredients:

1 (14- to 16-ounce) package super- or extra-firm tofu
1 teaspoon vegetable oil
2 tablespoons soy sauce
¼ teaspoon black pepper

MY TIPS:

Directions:

1. Place the unopened package of tofu in the freezer for at least 4 hours, or as long as 3 months.
2. Bring a pot of water to a boil. Remove the frozen tofu from its package and add it to the pot. Boil the tofu for 10 minutes.
3. Remove the tofu from the pot and let cool. When cool enough to handle, gently press the water out of the tofu with a clean kitchen towel. Be careful not to break the tofu.
4. Cut the tofu into ½-inch cubes and place in a medium bowl. Add the oil and mix until it's thoroughly coated. Add the soy sauce and pepper and mix again. Let the tofu marinate for 30 minutes (or longer) in the refrigerator.
5. Spread a single layer of tofu in your air fryer, making sure that the cubes don't touch. Set the temperature to 375 degrees and air-fry for 8 minutes. Remove the basket and shake it, then continue to air-fry until golden brown and crispy, another 4 to 7 minutes.
6. Serve right away, or store in an airtight container in the fridge for up to 5 days. To reheat, warm gently in a skillet on the stovetop. You can also microwave in a microwave-safe bowl in 30-second increments until hot, but it won't be as crispy.

TONI'S TIPS:

>>Fried tofu freezes great! Lay the cooked tofu cubes out on a baking sheet and freeze for 2 or 3 hours. Transfer the frozen tofu to an airtight container or freezer bag and freeze for up to 3 months. Thaw in the refrigerator overnight or in a microwave-safe bowl in the microwave in 30-second increments.

PERFECT PINTO BEANS

I love pinto beans—especially homemade! It's hard to compete with canned beans for convenience, but starting with dried beans means you can infuse them with tons of flavor while they cook (see my optional additions list for ideas). However, I can never seem to remember to take the time-saving step of soaking them in advance. If this sounds like you, too, give this recipe a try—no presoaking is required. I can eat a whole bowlful for dinner with nothing else and feel completely satisfied, but these beans also go great with my Mexican Rice (page 170), Pico de Gallo (page 194), Sheet Pan Fajitas (page 122), and Avocado Cream (page 192).

STOVETOP METHOD

Serves 6 to 8 | Ready in 2½ hours

Ingredients:

4 quarts water, divided
3 cups dried pinto beans
½ teaspoon salt, or to taste

Optional additions:

If you like spicy, add 1 minced jalapeño or a pinch of red chili flakes in step 2
Add 4 minced garlic cloves in step 2
Add ½ yellow onion, diced, in step 2
Add ¼ teaspoon ground cumin in step 2

Directions:

1. In a large pot, bring 2 quarts of the water to a boil over medium-high heat.
2. Add the pinto beans, salt, and any optional additions, cover, and cook for 45 minutes.
3. Add the remaining 2 quarts water, stir, and cover again with the lid. Lower the heat to medium and cook for 1 hour.
4. Check the beans; if they're not as soft as you like them, cover and cook for up to 30 minutes more.
5. Serve right away or store in an airtight container in the fridge for up to 5 days. To reheat, warm gently in a skillet on the stovetop, or microwave in a microwave-safe bowl in 30-second increments until hot.

PRESSURE COOKER METHOD

Serves 6 to 8 | Ready in 1 hour

Ingredients:

3 cups dried pinto beans
2 quarts water
½ teaspoon salt, or to taste

Optional additions:

If you like spicy, add 1 minced jalapeño or a pinch of red pepper flakes in step 1
Add 4 garlic cloves, minced, in step 1
Add ½ yellow onion, diced, in step 1
Add ¼ teaspoon ground cumin in step 1

Directions:

1. In a 6-quart pressure cooker, combine the beans, water, salt, and any optional additions that you're using. Cook on high pressure for 25 minutes.
2. Release the pressure with a quick release and remove the lid. Switch to the Sauté function and cook, stirring occasionally, until the beans reach your desired softness, 25 to 35 minutes.
3. Serve right away or store in an airtight container in the fridge for up to 5 days. To reheat, warm gently in a skillet on the stovetop, or microwave in a microwave-safe bowl in 30-second increments until hot.

TONI'S TIPS:

>>Homemade beans freeze surprisingly well! Allow them to cool completely, then package in airtight containers or freezer bags in 1½-cup portions (that's the amount normally in a can) with just enough liquid to cover them. They will keep for up to 3 months. Thaw in the refrigerator overnight or microwave in a microwave-safe bowl in 45-second increments.

If you have leftover broth from your beans, save it to add to your next pot of soup.

MY TIPS:

GARLIC EDAMAME

Serves 4 | Ready in 15 minutes

Edamame—also known as green soybeans—is a protein that you may recognize as a Japanese appetizer often served right in their pods. But they are more versatile than you may realize! I love shelled edamame in a bean salad, tossed into a stir-fry, or cooked up with a healthy dose of garlic in this savory recipe.

Ingredients:

1 teaspoon toasted sesame oil
1 (12-ounce) package frozen shelled edamame
3 garlic cloves, minced
1 tablespoon soy sauce
1 teaspoon sriracha or hot sauce

Optional additions and swaps:

If you don't have sesame oil, you can swap in vegetable oil; add ginger and more garlic for extra flavor
Add ½–1 teaspoon minced ginger or ¼ teaspoon ground ginger in step 2

Directions:

1. In a large skillet, heat the oil over medium-high heat. Add the frozen edamame and sauté until warmed through, 3 to 4 minutes.
2. Add the garlic, soy sauce, and sriracha and sauté until all the sauce is absorbed, 3 to 4 minutes.
3. Serve right away, or store in an airtight container in the fridge for up to 5 days. To reheat, warm gently in a skillet on the stovetop, or microwave in a microwave-safe bowl in 30-second increments until hot.

MY TIPS:

SOUTHWEST BLACK BEANS

Serves 4 | **Ready in 25 minutes**

Beans are a fantastic source of affordable protein. You can wrap these subtly spiced beans in a tortilla with brown rice, Avocado Cream (page 192), diced tomatoes, and some chopped lettuce, or add them to a bowl along with some quinoa, Calabacitas (page 158), salsa, and a side of tortilla chips. To save money, you can make these beans from scratch using my recipe for Perfect Pinto Beans (page 145) and using dried black beans instead of pintos.

Ingredients:

1 tablespoon vegetable oil
½ small red or yellow onion, diced
½ red or green bell pepper, diced
3 garlic cloves, minced
2 teaspoons ground cumin
1 teaspoon chili powder
2 (15-ounce) cans black beans, drained but not rinsed
1 teaspoon chipotle hot sauce
¼–½ teaspoon salt

Optional additions and swaps:

Swap the oil for ¼ cup water
For extra flavor, add ½ teaspoon garlic powder in step 2
For extra flavor, add ¼ teaspoon cayenne pepper in step 2

Directions:

1. In a large skillet, heat the oil over medium-high heat. Add the onion and bell pepper and sauté, stirring occasionally, until the bell pepper becomes tender, 5 to 6 minutes.
2. Add the garlic, cumin, and chili powder and cook, stirring, until fragrant, 1 to 2 minutes.
3. Add the beans and chipotle hot sauce, cover, lower the heat, and simmer for 10 minutes.
4. Serve right away, or store in an airtight container in the fridge for up to 5 days. To reheat, warm gently in a skillet on the stovetop, or microwave in a microwave-safe bowl in 30-second increments until hot.

TONI'S TIPS:

>>Beans were made for pressure-cooking! Throw everything except the oil into the pressure cooker and cook on high pressure for 3 minutes, then use a quick release.

TESTERS' TIPS:

>>"If cooking on the stovetop, stay by the pot in case your heat is too high and it cooks up quickly. If it begins to look dry, add water by the tablespoon until it reaches your desired consistency." —Janaye S. from Sunrise, FL

MY TIPS:

BASIC LENTILS

I cook up a big batch of these lentils to eat throughout the week and serve them in a variety of different ways: in a tortilla as a lentil hummus wrap, in a bowl with quinoa and Roasted Brussels Sprouts (page 154), or tossed into a bowl with steamed vegetables, "No Chicken" broth, and some cooked brown rice for a quick, nourishing soup.

PRESSURE COOKER METHOD

Serves 4 | Ready in 15 minutes

Ingredients:

1 cup green or brown lentils, rinsed

1½ cups water or vegetable broth

Directions:

1. In a 6-quart pressure cooker, combine the lentils and water or broth in the pressure cooker and cook on high pressure for 8 minutes.
2. Release the pressure with a quick release and remove the lid.
3. Serve right away or store in an airtight container in the fridge for up to 5 days. To reheat, warm gently in a skillet on the stovetop, or microwave in a microwave-safe bowl in 30-second increments until hot.

STOVETOP METHOD

Serves 4 | Ready in 40 minutes

Ingredients:

1 cup green or brown lentils, rinsed

1½ cups water or vegetable broth

Directions:

1. In a large pot, combine the lentils and water or broth. Bring to a boil over high heat. Cover the pot, reduce the heat to low, and simmer for 30 minutes.
2. Serve right away, or store in an airtight container in the fridge for up to 5 days. To reheat, warm gently in a skillet on the stovetop, or microwave in a microwave-safe bowl in 30-second increments until hot.

MY TIPS:

ROASTED BRUSSELS SPROUTS

Serves 2 to 4 | Ready in 55 minutes

Brussels sprouts have gotten a bad rap, but when they're roasted to crispy perfection instead of being boiled or steamed, you'll never have to persuade your kids or finicky dining partner to eat them again. In this recipe, they're oven-roasted (or cooked in the air fryer—see my tip!) and then quickly tossed in soy sauce and balsamic vinegar for an irresistibly savory finish.

Ingredients:

1 pound Brussels sprouts, trimmed and halved
3 tablespoons olive oil
3 garlic cloves, minced
⅛ teaspoon salt
Pinch black pepper
1 tablespoon soy sauce
1½ teaspoons balsamic vinegar

Directions:

1. Preheat the oven to 400 degrees. Line a rimmed baking sheet with aluminum foil, a silicone mat, or parchment paper.
2. In a large bowl, toss the Brussels sprouts with the olive oil, garlic, salt, and pepper until the Brussels sprouts are evenly coated.
3. Place the Brussels sprouts in a single layer on the prepared baking sheet. Bake for 35 to 45 minutes, until they look like they're getting crispy. (If your oven tends to bake faster, check at 25 minutes.)
4. Return the Brussels sprouts to the bowl and pour in the soy sauce and balsamic vinegar. Stir until evenly coated.
5. Serve immediately or store in an airtight container in the fridge for up to 4 days.

TONI'S TIPS:

>>If you want to cook these in the air fryer, use just 1 teaspoon oil. Place the Brussels sprout halves in a single layer in your air fryer. Set the temperature to 340 degrees and air-fry for 7 minutes. Remove the basket and shake it, then air-fry until golden brown and crispy, another 6 to 7 minutes. Continue to step 4.

TESTERS' TIPS:

>>"To save additional prep time, many grocery stores sell halved Brussels sprouts in 1-pound packages." —Justin A. from Sacramento, CA

MY TIPS:

ROASTED ROOT VEGGIES

Serves 4 to 6 | Ready in 1 hour

When autumn rolls around, my house starts filling up with the cozy aromas of hearty, versatile root veggies. Roasting root vegetables brings out their natural sugars for a caramelized effect that perfectly complements the savory flavors from the garlic and salt.

Ingredients:

2 large sweet potatoes, well scrubbed
3 large carrots, well scrubbed
1 large red onion, peeled
1 large beet, well scrubbed
12 garlic cloves, peeled
¼ cup olive oil
1 teaspoon salt

Optional additions and swaps:

Use only 2 tablespoon oil, or omit it entirely
Swap any root vegetables for other root vegetables (such as parsnip or rutabaga) or winter squash
Swap beet for golden beet for less mess
For extra flavor, swap the salt for garlic salt
Add ½–1 teaspoon dried thyme in step 3
Add 3 rosemary sprigs in step 3; remove before serving

Directions:

1. Preheat the oven to 400 degrees.
2. Cut the sweet potatoes, carrots, onion, and beet into 1-inch chunks or wedges.
3. Put all the vegetables and the whole garlic cloves on a rimmed baking sheet. Drizzle the oil and sprinkle on the salt. Stir until all the vegetables are evenly coated, then spread them out in a single layer.
4. Bake on the middle rack for 45 to 55 minutes, or until the veggies (especially the beets) are completely tender, stirring the vegetables halfway through.
5. Serve right away or store in an airtight container in the fridge for up to 4 days.

TESTERS' TIPS:

>>"If you love spice and lots of flavors, add about ¼ teaspoon each of harissa powder, Cajun seasoning, garlic powder, and onion powder." —Micah J. from Germany

MY TIPS:

CALABACITAS

Serves 4 to 6 | Ready in 30 minutes

I grew up eating my grandma's Calabacitas—zucchini, corn, and tomatoes in a spiced tomato broth with cheese—and this modified version takes me back. Besides tasting like comfort in a bowl, it's a fresh and flavorful way to use up your summer produce!

Ingredients:

1 tablespoon vegetable oil
1 small yellow onion, diced
3 small zucchini, halved lengthwise and sliced crosswise
2 Roma tomatoes, diced
3 garlic cloves, minced
1 (15.25-ounce) can corn kernels, drained and rinsed
½–1 teaspoon salt
¼ teaspoon dried oregano (preferably Mexican)
¼ teaspoon ground cumin
¼ teaspoon black pepper
A handful fresh cilantro, minced

Optional additions and swaps:

For spice, add 1 minced hot pepper (poblano, if in season) in step 1
For protein, add 1 (15-ounce) can black beans, drained and rinsed (1½ cups), in step 2
Swap the corn for hominy

Directions:

1. In a large skillet, heat the oil over medium-high heat Add the onion and sauté until tender and translucent, 1 to 2 minutes.
2. Add the zucchini, tomatoes, garlic, and corn and sauté, stirring occasionally, until the vegetables are slightly soft, about 5 minutes.
3. Stir in the salt, oregano, cumin, and black pepper and cook for another 1 to 2 minutes.
4. Stir in the cilantro and serve immediately, or store in an airtight container in the fridge for up to 4 days.

TESTERS' TIPS:

>>"Make use of your leftovers by adding them to a soup."
—Amber L. from Peoria, AZ

MY TIPS:

GARLIC ASPARAGUS AND MUSHROOMS

Serves 1 to 2 | Ready in 20 minutes

If you haven't yet tried asparagus and mushrooms together, you're missing out! Garlic brings out the best in both of them, and vegan butter gives this recipe extra richness. Besides enjoying them with a grain and your favorite plant-based protein in a mix-and-match bowl, this combo is also delicious as a pasta topping.

Ingredients:

2 tablespoons vegan butter
1 pound asparagus, trimmed and cut into 1-inch pieces
8 ounces cremini or button mushrooms, sliced
5 garlic cloves, minced
1/8 teaspoon salt

Optional additions and swaps:

Swap the vegan butter for vegetable oil
For spice, add a pinch of red chili flakes in step 3

Directions:

1. In a large skillet, melt the butter over medium-high heat. Add the asparagus and stir to coat it with the melted butter. Cover and cook until the asparagus is bright green and just beginning to turn tender, about 4 minutes.
2. Stir in the mushrooms. Cover and cook until the mushrooms start to soften, about 4 minutes.
3. Add the garlic and salt and sauté, stirring frequently, until the veggies are tender, 1 to 2 minutes.
4. Serve immediately, or store in an airtight container in the fridge for up to 5 days.

MY TIPS:

MASHED CAULIFLOWER

Serves 2 to 4 | Ready in 30 minutes

Cauliflower makes a great alternative to mashed potatoes on your Thanksgiving dinner table—or any other time of the year. Try pairing it with Roasted Root Vegetables (page 156) and Fried Tofu (page 142) for a plant-based winter feast. If you have the *Plant-Based on a Budget* cookbook, I recommend trying it topped with the Simple Gravy.

Ingredients:

1 cup vegetable broth
1 cup water
1 teaspoon salt, or to taste
1 head cauliflower, cut into ½-inch chunks (don't worry about keeping the florets intact)
2 tablespoons vegan butter, cut into ½-inch chunks
Black pepper, to taste

Optional additions and swaps:

Swap the vegan butter for more vegetable broth
Garnish with 1 teaspoon chopped fresh thyme

Directions:

1. In a large pot, bring the broth, water, and salt to a boil over medium-high heat. Add the cauliflower and bring it back to a boil. Cover, reduce the heat to low, and cook until the cauliflower is very tender, about 20 minutes.
2. Use a slotted spoon to transfer the cauliflower to a food processor. Add 3 tablespoons of the cooking liquid from the pot, along with the vegan butter. Process until smooth.
3. Taste and adjust the seasoning with salt and pepper.
4. Serve immediately, or store in an airtight container in the fridge for up to 4 days.

MY TIPS:

SPICED SWEET POTATO WEDGES

Serves 2 to 4 | Ready in 35 minutes

Sweet potatoes' vibrant orange hue signals that they're full of good-for-you beta carotene, but beyond their nutritional value, they're simply delicious. Besides enjoying them in your mix-and-match bowl, try them alongside your next veggie burger instead of French fries for a healthier treat.

Ingredients:

2 large sweet potatoes, well scrubbed and cut into ½-inch wedges
2 tablespoons olive oil
2 tablespoons potato starch
2 teaspoons taco seasoning (store-bought or page 122)
½ teaspoon salt

Directions:

1. Preheat the oven to 425 degrees. Line a rimmed baking sheet with a silicone mat or parchment paper.
2. In a large bowl, drizzle the potatoes with the oil, then sprinkle with the potato starch, taco seasoning, and salt. Mix thoroughly.
3. Spread the potatoes in a single layer on the prepared baking sheet and bake for 20 to 25 minutes, until fork-tender.
4. Serve immediately, or store in an airtight container in the fridge for up to 4 days.

MY TIPS:

QUINOA

Rinsing quinoa before cooking eliminates its mildly bitter flavor and yields a pot of fluffy grains (which are technically seeds, but that's beside the point). To rinse, use a fine-mesh strainer or a coffee filter, or, in a pinch, try lining a regular colander (the kind you use to drain pasta) with a clean kitchen towel.

PRESSURE COOKER METHOD

Makes 3 cups; serves 2 to 4 | Ready in 10 minutes

Ingredients:

1 cup quinoa
1½ cups water or vegetable broth

Directions:

1. Put the quinoa in a fine-mesh strainer and rinse under cool running water for at least 30 seconds.
2. Combine the quinoa and water or broth in the pressure cooker and cook on high pressure for 5 minutes.
3. Release the pressure with a quick release and remove the lid. Fluff the quinoa with a fork.
4. Serve right away, or store in an airtight container in the fridge for up to 1 week. To reheat, transfer the quinoa to a microwave-safe bowl and break up any large clumps. Cover with a damp paper towel and microwave for 30 seconds to 1 minute, until hot. Or, gently reheat in a skillet on the stove with a bit of water to prevent sticking.

STOVETOP METHOD

Makes 3 cups; serves 2 to 4 | Ready in 30 minutes

Ingredients:

1 cup quinoa
2 cups water or vegetable broth

Directions:

1. Put the quinoa in a fine-mesh strainer and rinse under cool running water for at least 30 seconds.
2. Combine the quinoa and water or broth in a medium pot and bring to a boil over

medium-high heat. Cover, reduce the heat to low, and cook until the liquid has been absorbed, about 20 minutes. Fluff the quinoa with a fork.

3. Serve right away, or store in an airtight container in the fridge for up to 1 week. To reheat, transfer the quinoa to a microwave-safe bowl and break up any large clumps. Cover with a damp paper towel and microwave for 30 seconds to 1 minute, until hot. Or gently reheat in a skillet on the stove with a bit of water to prevent sticking.

MY TIPS:

____

____

____

____

BROWN RICE

When I was a child, I lived with my Japanese grandfather and my Mexican grandmother. And although rice features prominently in both of their cultures' cuisines, brown rice is rarely used in either, so I wasn't introduced to it until later in life. In fact, I used to think it was a fancy rice for higher-end meals! Its texture is slightly rougher than white rice and it has more flavor, tasting almost nutty, so it brings more character to any dish. It's now one of my favorite grains.

PRESSURE COOKER METHOD

Serves 4 to 6 | Ready in 35 minutes

Ingredients:

1 cup brown rice
1½ cups water or vegetable broth

MY TIPS:

Directions:

1. Put the rice in a fine-mesh strainer and rinse under cool running water for at least 30 seconds.
2. Combine the rice and water or broth in the pressure cooker and cook on high pressure for 20 minutes.
3. Release the pressure with a quick release and remove the lid. Fluff the rice with a fork.
4. Serve immediately, or store the rice in an airtight container in the fridge for up to 5 days. To reheat, transfer the rice to a microwave-safe bowl and break up any large clumps. Add a small amount of water and cover the bowl with a damp paper towel. Microwave in 30-second increments until heated through. Or gently reheat the rice with a small amount of water in a small saucepan.

STOVETOP METHOD

Serves 4 to 6 | Ready in 50 minutes

Ingredients:

1 cup brown rice
2 cups water or vegetable broth

Directions:

1. Put the rice in a fine-mesh strainer and rinse under cool running water for at least 30 seconds.

2. Combine the rice and water or broth in a medium pot and bring to a boil over medium-high heat. Cover, reduce the heat to low, and cook until all the liquid has been absorbed, about 40 minutes. Fluff the rice with a fork.
3. Serve immediately, or store the rice in an airtight container in the fridge for up to 5 days. To reheat, transfer the rice to a microwave-safe bowl and break up any large clumps. Add a small amount of water and cover the bowl with a damp paper towel. Microwave in 30-second increments until heated through. Or gently reheat the rice with a small amount of water in a saucepan on the stove.

TONI'S TIPS:

>>For more flavor, you can stir in your favorite dried herbs, or cook with a bay leaf and some sautéed garlic and diced onion.

Allow the rice to cool completely, portion it out into individual servings, and freeze in airtight containers for up to 2 months. To thaw, microwave in a microwave-safe bowl for 2 to 3 minutes, or toss the frozen rice into a soup, stir-fry, or other dish.

MEXICAN RICE

Serves 8 | **Ready in 40 minutes**

If you've been part of my community for a while, you already know that I practically live off different variations of this rice. It's been a family favorite since I was a child, and now that I'm an adult, it continues to provide me with so much comfort.

Ingredients:

2 cups long-grain white rice
3 tablespoons vegetable oil
½ medium yellow onion, diced small
3 large garlic cloves, minced
3¾ cups vegetable or "No Chicken" broth
1 (8-ounce) can tomato sauce
1 teaspoon salt
Black pepper, to taste

Optional additions and swaps:

Swap the oil for an additional ¼ cup vegetable or "No Chicken" broth
For more nutrients, add ¾ cup frozen peas and carrots in step 2
For a little extra flavor, add a pinch of ground cumin in step 2
Stir in a handful of minced fresh cilantro when ready to serve

Directions:

1. Put the rice in a fine-mesh strainer and rinse under cool running water for at least 30 seconds.
2. In a medium pot, heat the oil over medium-high heat. Add the onion, garlic, and rice and sauté, stirring frequently, until some of the grains of rice begin to turn golden brown, 4 to 5 minutes.
3. Add the broth, tomato sauce, salt, and pepper and stir. Bring the mixture to a boil, then cover, reduce the heat to low, and simmer until the liquid has been absorbed, about 20 minutes. Fluff the rice with a fork.
4. Serve right away or store in an airtight container in the fridge for up to 5 days. To reheat, transfer the rice to a microwave-safe bowl and break up any large clumps. Add a small amount of water and cover the bowl with a damp paper towel. Microwave in 30-second increments until heated through. Or gently reheat the rice with a small amount of water in a saucepan on the stove.

TONI'S TIPS:

>>This rice can be made in a pressure cooker, but it does change the consistency a bit. Use the Sauté function for step 1, then add the remaining ingredients and cook on high

pressure for 5 minutes with a natural release. Fluff the rice with a fork and let it sit for 5 more minutes with the lid off to become more fluffy.

MY TIPS:

AMARANTH

Amaranth is a lot like quinoa, only its grains are even tinier! Also like quinoa, amaranth is technically a seed, but it is generally referred to as a grain and can be used as such in bowls, salads, pilafs, and porridges. But unlike quinoa, amaranth doesn't need to be rinsed before cooking.

PRESSURE COOKER METHOD

Serves 4 to 6 | Ready in 20 minutes

Ingredients:

1 cup amaranth
1½ cups water or vegetable broth

Directions:

1. Combine the amaranth and water or broth in the pressure cooker and cook on high pressure for 12 minutes.
2. Release the pressure with a quick release and remove the lid. Fluff the amaranth with a fork.
3. Serve right away, or store in an airtight container in the fridge for up to 1 week. To reheat, transfer the amaranth to a microwave-safe bowl and break up any clumps. Add a small amount of water and cover the bowl with a damp paper towel. Microwave in 30-second increments until heated through. Or, gently reheat the amaranth with a small amount of water in a small saucepan on the stove.

STOVETOP METHOD

Serves 4 to 6 | Ready in 35 minutes

Ingredients:

1 cup amaranth
2 cups water or vegetable broth

Directions:

1. Combine the amaranth and water or broth in a medium pot and bring to a boil over medium-high heat. Cover, reduce the heat to low, and cook until the liquid has been absorbed, about 20 minutes. Fluff the amaranth with a fork.

2. Serve right away, or store in an airtight container in the fridge for up to 1 week. To reheat, transfer the amaranth to a microwave-safe bowl and break up any clumps. Add a small amount of water and cover the bowl with a damp paper towel. Microwave in 30-second increments until heated through. Or, gently reheat the amaranth with a small amount of water in a small saucepan on the stove.

MY TIPS:

____

____

____

PEARL BARLEY

Barley—specifically pearl barley—has a pleasantly chewy texture and brims with fiber, and it boasts an impressive amount of calcium, too. The individual grains are a bit bigger than rice, so it will make your bowls, stir-fries, soups, and salads feel extra-substantial.

PRESSURE COOKER METHOD

Serves 4 to 6 | Ready in 30 minutes

Ingredients:

1 cup pearl barley

2 cups water or vegetable broth

Directions:

1. Combine the barley and water or broth in the pressure cooker and cook on high pressure for 20 minutes.
2. Release the pressure with a quick release and remove the lid. Fluff the barley with a fork.
3. Serve right away, or store in an airtight container in the fridge for up to 1 week. To reheat, transfer the barley to a microwave-safe bowl and break up any clumps. Add a small amount of water and cover the bowl with a damp paper towel. Microwave in 30-second increments until heated through. Or, gently reheat the barley with a small amount of water in a small saucepan on the stove.

STOVETOP METHOD

Serves 4 to 6 | Ready in 40 minutes

Ingredients:

1 cup pearl barley

3 cups water

Directions:

1. Combine the barley and water or broth in a medium pot and bring to a boil over medium-high heat. Cover, reduce the heat to low, and cook until the liquid has been absorbed, about 30 minutes. Fluff with a fork.

2. Serve right away, or store in an airtight container in the fridge for up to 1 week. To reheat, transfer the barley to a microwave-safe bowl and break up any clumps. Add a small amount of water and cover the bowl with a damp paper towel. Microwave in 30-second increments until heated through. Or, gently reheat the barley with a small amount of water in a small saucepan on the stove.

MY TIPS:

____

____

____

____

TORTILLAS DE HARINA (FLOUR TORTILLAS)

Makes 10 tortillas | Ready in 1 hour 15 minutes

When I was a child, I used to love making homemade tortillas with my grandma. She'd let me roll out the soft, pliable dough and give me cookie cutters to cut it into whatever holiday shapes I wanted. Although I no longer make them every day, they're so easy and cheap to make, plus they taste 100 times better than any variety you'll find in the store. And best of all, they don't contain lard!

Ingredients

- 2½–3 cups all-purpose flour, plus more for dusting
- ⅓ cup vegan butter (preferably unsalted)
- ½ teaspoon baking powder
- 1 teaspoon salt
- 1 cup hot water

Directions:

1. In a large bowl, use your hands to combine 2½ cups flour and the vegan butter, making sure to massage all the clumps of shortening into the flour. I usually continuously rub my hands in a back-and-forth motion to feel that all the butter particles have been broken up. If the dough feels like it's too wet and sticky, try adding up to ½ cup more flour by the tablespoon. When it seems that they're well combined, mix in the baking powder.
2. Dissolve the salt in the hot water and pour two-thirds of it into the flour mixture, then mix with your hands. Add another teaspoon or so of the remaining water if there are still loose flour particles. The dough should be smooth, not sticky.
3. Divide the dough into 10 equal balls. Cover them with a damp warm kitchen towel and let them rest for 30 minutes.
4. After the dough has rested, roll out each ball of dough on a lightly floured work surface to about ¼ inch thick. Continue to lightly flour the dough if it begins to stick.

5. Heat a nonstick griddle or skillet over medium-high heat. Once hot, cook the tortillas one at a time, until it bubbles and has brown spots on the bottom, about 45 seconds. Flip the tortilla over and cook the other side. Transfer to a plate and cover with a towel while you cook the remaining tortillas.
6. Serve immediately.

TONI'S TIP:

>>You can freeze these tortillas in a freezer bag for up to 2 months. Allow them to cool completely, separate each tortilla with parchment paper in between, place in the bag, and press out the air.

MY TIPS:

SESAME GINGER DRESSING

Makes ½ cup | Ready in 5 minutes

Two classic flavors from East Asian cuisine combine for a scrumptious dressing you can pour over salads, grains, and steamed or roasted vegetables, or even use as a dipping sauce for dumplings or spring rolls.

Ingredients:

1 tablespoon minced ginger
2 tablespoons olive oil
2 tablespoons soy sauce
2 tablespoons rice vinegar
1½ tablespoons maple syrup
1 tablespoon toasted sesame oil

Optional additions and swaps:

Use only 1½ teaspoons oil
Swap the maple syrup for agave
Add ½–1 teaspoon sriracha
Add ½–1 teaspoon sesame seeds

Directions:

1. In a small bowl, whisk together all the ingredients until well combined. You can also put it in a mason jar and shake it.
2. Store in an airtight container in the fridge for up to 1 week.

MY TIPS:

PEANUT SAUCE

Makes about ¾ cup | Ready in 10 minutes

This sauce is fantastic served with Fried Tofu (page 142), some steamed vegetables, and brown rice. It's also the base for my Udon Noodles with Peanut Sauce (page 94), which can be paired with fresh spring rolls (I recommend the ones in *The Friendly Vegan Cookbook*).

Ingredients:

¼ cup smooth peanut butter

2 large garlic cloves, minced

1½ teaspoons minced ginger

3 tablespoons water

1 tablespoon agave or maple syrup

1 tablespoon soy sauce

1 tablespoon rice vinegar

Optional additions and swaps:

Swap the minced garlic for ¼ teaspoon garlic powder

Swap the fresh ginger for ¼ teaspoon ground ginger

For spice, add a splash of sriracha, some minced hot pepper, or a pinch of red chili flakes

For a thinner sauce, add another 1 tablespoon water

Directions:

1. In a medium bowl, whisk together all the ingredients for 1 to 2 minutes, or until well blended.
2. Store in an airtight container in the refrigerator for up to 1 week.

TESTERS' TIPS:

>>"My family enjoyed this with portobello mushrooms, sautéed spinach, and brown rice." —Caryn G. from Arlington, VA

MY TIPS:

TAHINI DRESSING

Makes about ¾ cup | Ready in 5 minutes

When puréed, sesame seeds transform into a thick and decadent paste known as tahini. It's surprisingly high in calcium and potassium and is one of the key ingredients in Middle Eastern spreads like hummus and baba ghanoush. This multipurpose dressing will take you as far as your imagination can travel, but I enjoy pairing it with fresh and cooked vegetables, potatoes, or rice.

Ingredients:

¼ cup tahini
1 garlic clove, minced
Pinch salt and black pepper
2 tablespoons lemon juice
2 tablespoons maple syrup
2 tablespoons water

Optional additions:

Add 1 tablespoon olive oil
Add a pinch of red chili flakes
If you like a thinner dressing, add another 1–2 tablespoons water
If you prefer a less sweet dressing, start with 1 tablespoon maple syrup

Directions:

1. In a small bowl, whisk together all the ingredients until well combined.
2. Store in an airtight container in the fridge for up to 1 week.

MY TIPS:

MAPLE MUSTARD DRESSING

Makes about ¾ cup | Ready in 5 minutes

Just thinking about this sweet and savory dressing makes my mouth water! It's great on so many different bowls, but I especially like it with brown rice, roasted butternut squash, and garbanzo beans.

Ingredients:

¼ cup Dijon mustard
¼ cup apple cider vinegar
3 tablespoons maple or agave syrup
2 tablespoons olive oil
2 garlic cloves, minced
Black pepper, to taste

Optional additions:

For extra sweetness, add another 1 tablespoon maple or agave syrup
For less acidity, use only 3 tablespoons apple cider vinegar

Directions:

1. In a small bowl, whisk together all the ingredients until well combined. You can also put it in a mason jar and shake it.
2. Store in an airtight container in the fridge for up to 1 week.

MY TIPS:

CLASSIC BALSAMIC VINAIGRETTE

Makes about ¾ cup | Ready in 5 minutes

Balsamic vinegar is a dark, tangy-sweet vinegar that originates in Italy, where it is aged for years in wooden barrels, giving it a unique and complex flavor. When you want to take your plain dinner salad to the next level, reach for this dressing.

Ingredients:

½ cup extra virgin olive oil
¼ cup balsamic vinegar
1½ teaspoons Dijon mustard
1 teaspoon agave
⅛ teaspoon garlic powder

Optional addition:

For extra sweetness, add another ½–1 teaspoon agave

Directions:

1. In a small bowl, whisk together all the ingredients until well combined.
2. Store in an airtight container in the fridge for up to 1 week.

MY TIPS:

TOMATILLO SALSA

Makes 2 cups | Ready in 30 minutes

During the summer, when tomatillos are in abundance, we use this salsa on everything—adding it to a breakfast burrito, a bowl with lentils and quinoa, a chopped vegetable salad, or a veggie taco. If you're new to tomatillos, note that you'll want to remove the papery husks and rinse the fruit itself until it's no longer sticky.

Ingredients:

2 pounds tomatillos, husked and rinsed
1 large poblano, halved and seeded
½ medium white or yellow onion, thickly sliced
5 garlic cloves, peeled
Vegetable oil spray
1 tablespoon ground cumin
2 teaspoons ground coriander
½ cup packed fresh cilantro
¾ teaspoon salt, or to taste

Optional additions and swaps:

For spice, add 1–2 whole serranos or jalapeños in step 2
Swap the vegetable oil spray for 1–2 teaspoons vegetable oil
For a creamier salsa, add 1 ripe avocado, peeled and pitted, in step 5

Directions:

1. Arrange the top oven rack so that it's about 6 inches from the heating element. Turn on the broiler. Line a rimmed baking sheet with a silicone mat or parchment paper.
2. Place the tomatillos on one side of the prepared baking sheet and the poblano, onion slices, and garlic cloves on the other. (The tomatillos may need extra time under the broiler.) Spray the veggies with oil and then sprinkle with the cumin and coriander.
3. Broil for 4 to 5 minutes, until the veggies start bubbling. Make sure to keep an eye on them so they don't burn.
4. Take the baking sheet out of the oven, flip all of the ingredients, and broil for another 4 to 5 minutes, or until the ingredients look nicely charred. If the tomatillos need some extra time, remove everything else and continue to broil them until charred.
5. Allow to cool for 5 to 10 minutes, then transfer all the broiled ingredients and their juices to a food processor or blender, add the cilantro and salt, and blend until smooth.
6. Store in an airtight container in the fridge for up to 1 week.

TONI'S TIPS:

>>This recipe works great in an air fryer. Place the tomatillos, poblano, onion, and garlic in a single layer in the air fryer basket. Spray with oil and sprinkle with the cumin and coriander. Set the temperature to 390 degrees and air-fry for 5 minutes, then flip the ingredients and air-fry for 5 more minutes. Continue with step 5.

MY TIPS:

CASHEW CREMA

Makes about 1¾ cups | Ready in 5 minutes

For an ultra-rich and creamy sauce, nothing beats the humble cashew. When soaked in water and blended until smooth, the nuts are transformed into a decadent cream that you can use exactly as you would sour cream: on baked potatoes, stirred into noodles, or as a dipping sauce for vegetables.

Ingredients:

1 cup raw cashews, rinsed, soaked overnight, and drained

¼ teaspoon salt

½ cup + 2 tablespoons water

1½ tablespoons lemon juice

Optional addition:

To make it a little sourer, add an extra ¼ teaspoon salt

Directions:

1. Combine the soaked cashews, salt, water, and lemon juice in a high-powered blender or food processor. Blend until creamy, about 5 minutes. (You can alternatively use a standard blender, but it will take longer depending on your blender's strength. Keep blending until the crema is smooth and there are no bits of cashew left.)
2. Store in an airtight container in the fridge for up to 1 week.

TONI'S TIPS:

>>If you're shopping in the bulk section and have the option of cashew pieces or whole cashews, choose the pieces, which are almost always less expensive and work just as well in this recipe.

MY TIPS:

AVOCADO CREAM

Makes about 1½ cups | Ready in 10 minutes

Avocado Cream always reminds me of my talented friend Dinorah. She's not only a singer with a stunningly beautiful voice (she sang at my wedding!), but she is also an incredible cook who introduced me to Avocado Cream when she served it at her house with nopales and rice. It's also great on tacos, as a dip, in a burrito, on nachos, or on a Mexican-inspired bowl. Where there is a range of measurements in this ingredients list, start with the smaller amounts, taste, and add more based on your preferences.

Ingredients:

4 small avocados or 2 large avocados, peeled and pitted
¼ cup chopped red or yellow onion
3–4 small garlic cloves, peeled
½–1 tablespoon minced fresh cilantro
1 tablespoon lemon juice
½–1 teaspoon salt

Optional addition:

Add ½ small jalapeño, for spice

Directions:

1. In a food processor or blender, process all the ingredients on high until completely creamy, scraping down the sides of the bowl if avocado gets stuck.
2. Serve immediately.

TESTERS' TIPS:

>>"You can change it up by adding a dollop of vegan sour cream, adding a pinch of chili powder or garlic powder, or doubling the lemon juice." —Lisa W. from Denver, CO

MY TIPS:

PICO DE GALLO

Makes about 1½ cups | Ready in 10 minutes

This is one of the most-used toppings in our home. If you like spice, I highly recommend adding some minced hot peppers to get your mouth tingling. Spicy or not, it's the ideal accompaniment to a simple dish of rice and beans, as a dip for tortilla chips, or spooned over your favorite nachos.

Ingredients:

2 large tomatoes, diced (about 2 cups)

½ yellow or white onion, finely diced (about ¾ cup)

¼ cup packed fresh cilantro, minced

Juice of 1 lime

Salt, to taste

Optional additions and swaps:

Add 1 large avocado, peeled, pitted, and diced

For spice, add 1 serrano or small jalapeño, minced

Add 2 small garlic cloves, minced

Swap the lime for ½ lemon

Directions:

1. In a small bowl, combine all the ingredients and mix well.
2. Store in an airtight container in the fridge for up to 3 days.

MY TIPS:

MAKE-AND-TAKE SNACKS

Having healthy homemade snacks on hand means it's less likely that we'll reach for packaged products filled with excessive sugar, salt, and fat when we're feeling peckish. I like to make these in bulk so that they'll last throughout the week and to have something for guests to nibble on when they stop by. For optimal freshness, store your snacks in airtight glass containers in a cool, dry place.

CINNAMON SPICED NUTS

Makes 1½ cups | Ready in 15 minutes

This is an updated version of a holiday classic that I like to make all year round. The nuts are sweetened with maple syrup instead of sugar and seasoned with just the right amount of cinnamon. For a little heat, try adding a pinch of cayenne to the mix before popping in the oven.

Ingredients:

1½ cups your choice raw nuts (pecans, almonds, walnuts, etc.)
1½ tablespoons maple syrup
1 teaspoon ground cinnamon

Optional addition:

For heat, add a pinch of cayenne pepper in step 2

Directions:

1. Preheat the oven to 300 degrees. Line a rimmed baking sheet with parchment paper or a silicone mat.
2. In a medium bowl, stir together the nuts, maple syrup, and cinnamon until thoroughly combined.
3. Spread out the nuts in a single layer on the prepared baking sheet. Bake for 10 minutes, or until lightly browned. Let the nuts cool on the baking sheet.
4. Store in an airtight container at room temperature for up to 1 month.

MY TIPS:

TRAIL MIX

Makes 3¼ cups | Ready in 5 minutes

I love how versatile trail mix can be. I usually base mine on whichever nuts or seeds I have on hand in my pantry, or whatever happens to be on sale when I go shopping! This keeps it interesting and allows me to flex my creative muscles in the kitchen.

Ingredients:

¾ cup your choice roasted or raw nuts (almonds, cashews, hazelnuts, macadamias, peanuts, pecans, shelled pistachios, walnuts)
¾ cup your second choice of nuts
½ cup your choice of seeds (sunflower, pumpkin, squash, hemp)
½ cup your second choice of seeds
½ cup your favorite dried fruit
¼ cup vegan chocolate chips

Directions:

Combine all the ingredients in an airtight container, mason jar, or reusable bag. Stir or shake to incorporate. As long as your nuts are fresh, the trail mix can be stored at room temperature for up to 2 months.

MY TIPS:

KALE CHIPS

Serves 2 to 4 | Ready in 20 minutes

Found some wilted kale in the back of your fridge? Give those tired greens some new life and prevent food waste with this easy and super-tasty recipe. You'll never be tempted to buy expensive packaged kale chips ever again!

Ingredients:

1 large bunch curly kale, washed and completely dried

1 tablespoon vegetable oil

1–2 pinches salt

Optional additions:

Add a few pinches nutritional yeast with the salt in step 4

Add a few pinches garlic powder with the salt in step 4

Add a few pinches red chili flakes with the salt in step 4

Add a pinch paprika with the salt in step 4

Directions:

1. Preheat the oven to 350 degrees. Line a rimmed baking sheet with a silicone mat or parchment paper.
2. Remove the kale stems and cut the leaves into 2-inch pieces. (You should have about 4 cups.)
3. Put the kale in a large bowl. Pour on the oil and gently massage it into the leaves for 1 minute.
4. Spread out the kale in a single layer on the prepared baking sheet and sprinkle on a pinch or two of salt. Bake for 8 to 10 minutes, until the kale is crispy and lightly browned at the edges.
5. Serve immediately or let the chips cool and store in a paper bag at room temperature for up to 1 week.

TONI'S TIPS:

>>This recipe was destined for the air fryer! Prep the kale as instructed (you can decrease the oil to 1½ teaspoons if you like), then put the kale in the air fryer. Set the temperature for 350 degrees and air-fry for 5 minutes.

TESTERS' TIPS:

>>"Save time by buying packaged pre-cut and washed kale." —Mary D. from West Chester, PA

>>"Make sure to dry the kale completely after washing it or the oil won't stick to the kale." —Jami G. from La Crosse, WI

MY TIPS:

PINTO BEAN DIP

Makes 1 cup | Ready in 5 minutes

This bean dip is incredibly easy to prepare, full of flavor, and surprisingly versatile. Try pairing it with chips, dollop some into a burrito, stuff it into a crunchy tortilla shell, or use it as a spread for toast or crackers for a filling snack.

Ingredients:

1 (15-ounce) can pinto beans, drained and rinsed
⅓ cup red or green salsa
½–1 jalapeño or serrano pepper, chopped
3 tablespoons nutritional yeast
2 teaspoons ground cumin
1 teaspoon garlic powder
1 teaspoon onion powder
⅛ teaspoon salt, or to taste

Optional swap:

Swap the spices for 1 tablespoon taco seasoning (store-bought or page 122)

Directions:

1. Combine all the ingredients in a food processor or blender and process until completely creamy.
2. Serve right away or store in an airtight container in the refrigerator for up to 5 days.

TESTERS' TIPS:

>>"For extra flavor, add a small amount of sautéed onion before processing." —Diane D. from Annapolis, MD

MY TIPS:

TAPENADE

Makes about 1½ cups | Ready in 10 minutes

Perfect for parties, this tasty spread comes together in less than 10 minutes and is bursting with tart and tangy Mediterranean flavors. Serve with your favorite dippers—we like pita chips, baked sourdough slices, crackers, cucumber slices, and more!

Ingredients:

1 (6-ounce) jar whole or sliced Manzanilla olives, drained

½ cup whole or sliced kalamata olives, drained

1½ tablespoons fresh flat-leaf parsley

1 tablespoon drained capers

1 large garlic clove, peeled

Optional additions and swaps:

For spice, add ¼–½ teaspoon red chili flakes

For more tang, add 1½ teaspoons lemon juice

For a cheaper option, swap the Manzanilla and/or kalamata for green olives

Directions:

1. Combine all the ingredients in a food processor and pulse 8 to 10 times, until the ingredients are chunky and well chopped but not puréed. Scrape down the sides of the food processor as needed.
2. Serve immediately or store in an airtight container in the refrigerator for up to 7 days.

TONI'S TIPS:

>>If you don't have a food processor, you can make this in your blender by pulsing.

MY TIPS:

DATE BARS

Makes 8 bars | Ready in 40 minutes

Stash these in your bag for busy days when you know you'll need a snack, try them in the morning for a quick breakfast, or enjoy them when it's time to refuel on your next hike or bike ride.

Ingredients:

½ cup creamy peanut butter
1 cup pitted Medjool dates
1 cup old-fashioned oats
2 tablespoons maple syrup
¼ cup raisins

Optional additions and swaps:

For some crunch, add 2 tablespoons chopped nuts of your choice in step 3
Swap the raisins for dried cranberries

Directions:

1. In a small, microwave-safe bowl, microwave the peanut butter for 30 seconds. Mix with a fork until smooth. (If the peanut butter is still lumpy, microwave in 20-second increments, mixing in between, until completely smooth.)
2. Transfer the peanut butter to a food processor, add the dates, and process until smooth.
3. Carefully remove the blade and add the remaining ingredients. (Or, if you are using a small food processor, transfer the mixture to a medium bowl and add the remaining ingredients.) Using a wooden spoon or a strong silicone spatula, mix everything well.
4. Transfer the mixture to an 8-inch baking pan. Use a piece of parchment paper to evenly press it into the pan. Refrigerate for 30 minutes.
5. Cut into 8 bars. Store in an airtight container in the refrigerator for up to 10 days or in the freezer for up to 2 months.

TONI'S TIPS:

>>No microwave? No problem! Place a small pot of water over medium-low heat with a metal or heat-safe glass bowl resting on top of it (make sure the bowl doesn't touch the water). Put the peanut butter in the bowl and stir frequently until completely melted. Monitor closely to avoid burning.

TESTERS' TIPS:

>>"These are also great rolled into bite-size balls." —Taylor R. from Chattanooga, TN

MY TIPS:

CRISPY GARBANZO BEANS

Serves 1½ cups | Ready in 20 minutes

Never underestimate the power of the garbanzo bean, aka chickpea! They are healthy, delicious, and super-satiating, and this recipe showcases their remarkable versatility. I like to eat these right out of the bowl, but they also make amazing salad toppers.

Ingredients:

1 (15-ounce) can garbanzo beans, drained and rinsed
1 tablespoon olive oil

Seasoning options:

1 teaspoon taco seasoning (store-bought or page 122)
1 teaspoon garlic powder + ⅛ teaspoon salt
1½ teaspoons brown sugar + ½ teaspoon ground cinnamon
Your favorite homemade or store-bought spice blend

Directions:

1. Preheat the oven to 425 degrees. Line a rimmed baking sheet with parchment paper or a silicone mat.
2. Lay a clean towel or paper towel on the baking sheet and pour the garbanzo beans on top. Place another clean towel or paper towel on top of the garbanzo beans and blot them dry. Once the beans are completely dry, remove the towels.
3. Remove any skins that are coming off the beans. Drizzle on the oil and shake the pan until the beans are evenly coated.
4. Bake for 12 minutes, shake the pan, and bake for another 13 minutes. If you prefer even crispier bean, shake again and bake for 5 more minutes.
5. Pour the beans into a bowl and stir in your favorite seasoning. Store in an uncovered bowl at room temperature for up to 3 days.

MY TIPS:

SIMPLE DESSERTS

For the longest time, I thought of myself as more of a savory person than one who preferred sweets. I'm not sure when that changed, but I now have a huge sweet tooth, and these are some of my favorite indulgent treats.

CHOCOLATE-DIPPED STUFFED DATES

Makes 6 dates | **Ready in 1 hour**

Of all the desserts in this chapter, this one gets the most game time in our home. Reminiscent of packaged caramel-chocolate candy bars, these Chocolate-Dipped Stuffed Dates are quick and easy to make, and they taste *way* better than any vending machine candy could hope to!

Ingredients:

6 Medjool dates
¼ cup creamy or crunchy nut butter
⅓ cup vegan chocolate chips

Optional additions:

Top with 1 tablespoon chopped nuts
Top with 1 tablespoon unsweetened shredded coconut
Garnish with a pinch of sea salt
Drizzle with melted nut butter

Directions:

1. Cut a slit down the length of each date and remove the pits.
2. Fill the center of each date with a spoonful of nut butter.
3. In a medium microwave-safe bowl, microwave the chocolate chips for 45 seconds. Mix with a fork until smooth. (If the chocolate is still lumpy, microwave in 20-second increments, mixing in between, until completely smooth.)
4. Dip half of each stuffed date into the melted chocolate. Transfer to a plate lined with parchment paper or a silicone baking mat.
5. Place in the freezer for at least 30 minutes and enjoy frozen. Store the dates in an airtight container in the freezer for up to 2 months. If you like them to be softer when you eat them, thaw for 10 minutes on the counter.

TESTERS' TIPS:

>>"If your dates are squished, try dipping them in melted peanut butter, freezing them, and then dipping in chocolate and freezing again." —Jill S. from Tiffin, IA

>>"If you want to speed up the process, instead of dipping the dates in melted chocolate, push 2 or 3 individual chocolate chips into the peanut butter before freezing the dates." —Megan L. from Pittsburgh, PA

MY TIPS:

BAKED PEARS

Serves 6 | Ready in 40 minutes

Despite being incredibly simple to whip up, these Baked Pears look and taste like an elegant dessert you'd find on the menu at a fancy restaurant. To make them extra decadent, serve with vegan vanilla ice cream or a big spoonful of Coconut Whipped Cream from the *Plant-Based on a Budget* cookbook.

Ingredients:

¼ cup + 2 tablespoons chopped walnuts and/or pecans

4–5 tablespoons raisins and/or dried cranberries

¾ teaspoon pumpkin pie spice (store-bought or see Toni's Tips below), plus more for sprinkling

4–5 tablespoons agave and/or maple syrup, plus more for drizzling

3 ripe pears, halved

Directions:

1. Preheat the oven to 350 degrees. Line a rimmed baking sheet with parchment paper or a silicone mat.
2. In a bowl, mix together the nuts, dried fruit, pumpkin pie spice, and agave or maple syrup until well combined.
3. On the rounded side of each pear half, slice away a tiny sliver of skin to create a flat base so they don't rock back and forth on the baking sheet.
4. Using a melon baller or spoon, scoop out the core of the pears. Add a generous scoop of nut mixture to each pear half. If you'd like to drizzle on a little more sweetener or sprinkle on a bit more pumpkin pie spice, feel free.
5. Bake for 25 minutes, or until softened and tender. If your pears weren't ripe to begin with, you may need to add more time.

TONI'S TIPS:

>>If you don't have store-bought pumpkin pie spice, it's easy to DIY. Combine 1 tablespoon ground cinnamon, 1½ teaspoons ground ginger, 1 teaspoon ground cloves, ½ teaspoon ground nutmeg, and ⅛ teaspoon ground allspice (optional) in a small jar. Store in a cool, dry place until you're ready to use the spice blend. I use this spice blend in so many different ways, including adding it to pancake batter, muffin mixes, and banana bread. Experimenting is half the fun—eating is the other half!

TESTERS' TIPS:

>>"Adding 1/4 cup quick oats to the nut and fruit topping takes this from a dessert to a breakfast item. Serve with some vegan yogurt." —Amanda M. from Santa Rosa, CA

MY TIPS:

APPLE CRISP

Serves 8 to 9 | **Ready in 1 hour**

In the fall, I use fresh apples for this crisp, but in the summer when stone fruits are in peak season, I swap out the apples for ripe peaches. Whatever fruit you choose, try serving this dessert warm with vegan vanilla ice cream for a divinely decadent experience.

Ingredients:

3 large apples, cored and thinly sliced
¾ cup brown sugar, divided, plus more for sprinkling
½ cup all-purpose flour
½ cup quick oats
1 teaspoon salt
1 teaspoon ground cinnamon
1 teaspoon ground allspice
1 teaspoon vanilla extract
½ cup vegan butter, melted

Optional swaps:

Replace the apples with pears, peaches, or plums
If you don't have allspice, double the cinnamon
Omit the brown sugar in step 2

Directions:

1. Preheat the oven to 350 degrees. Grease an 8-inch baking dish.
2. Put the sliced apples in the prepared baking dish and mix in ¼ cup of the brown sugar.
3. In a separate bowl, combine the remaining ½ cup brown sugar, flour, oats, salt, cinnamon, allspice, vanilla, and melted butter. Mix until well combined.
4. Spoon the oat mixture on top the apples and spread evenly. Sprinkle with more brown sugar if you like.
5. Bake for 45 to 55 minutes, or until the topping is crisp and brown and the apples are tender.

MY TIPS:

BANANA ICE CREAM (3 WAYS)

This smooth and creamy frozen dessert doesn't require a lot of ingredients to prepare, but it does require some planning ahead! You'll want to make sure to freeze your bananas overnight. Once everything is in the blender, it can take up to 5 minutes to achieve its luscious texture. To serve, scoop the ice cream right into bowls or ice cream cones and enjoy!

BANANA ICE CREAM

Serves 2 | Ready in 5 minutes

There's a lot to be said for simplicity! This banana ice cream is creamy and naturally sweet. The optional vanilla extract and agave syrup give it a boost, but it's also delicious on its own.

Ingredients:

3 ripe bananas, thinly sliced and frozen

Optional additions:

Add a splash of plant-based milk
Add 1½ teaspoons agave
Add ½ teaspoon vanilla extract

Directions:

1. In a food processor or high-powered blender, pulse or blend the frozen banana slices and any optional ingredients until you have thick, creamy ice cream.
2. Serve immediately.

STRAWBERRY BANANA ICE CREAM

Serves 2 | **Ready in 5 minutes**

This variation is just bursting with summery strawberry flavor. If you like, serve it topped with extra sliced berries.

Ingredients:

2 ripe bananas, thinly sliced and frozen
2 cups frozen strawberries

Optional additions:

Add 1/4 cup plant-based milk
Add 1 tablespoon agave
Add 1/2 teaspoon vanilla extract

Directions:

1. In a food processor or high-powered blender, pulse or blend the frozen banana slices, strawberries, and any optional ingredients until you have thick, creamy ice cream.
2. Serve immediately.

MY TIPS:

CHOCOLATE PB BANANA ICE CREAM

Serves 2 | **Ready in 5 minutes**

I *love* the classic combo of chocolate and peanut butter—as you might notice from looking at other recipes in this chapter! This decadent banana ice cream is extra nice with some chopped nuts and a little vegan whipped cream on top.

Ingredients:

3 ripe bananas, thinly sliced and frozen
3 tablespoons creamy peanut butter
1 tablespoon cocoa powder

Optional additions:

Add ¼ cup plant-based milk
Add 1 tablespoon agave
Add ½ teaspoon vanilla extract

Directions:

1. In a food processor or high-powered blender, pulse or blend the frozen banana slices, peanut butter, cocoa powder, and any optional ingredients until you have thick, creamy ice cream.
2. Serve immediately.

TONI'S TIPS:

>>If you have a Vitamix or other high-speed blender, you won't need to use any plant-based milk for this recipe. But if you're using a standard or immersion blender, you can add milk a tablespoon at a time until it's completely smooth.
>>If you want your ice cream's texture to be a little firmer, spoon it into a loaf pan or storage container and freeze for 45 minutes to an hour before scooping.

TESTERS' TIPS:

>>"This works great in a food processor. Add about ¼ cup plant-based milk to the plain banana ice cream, ⅓ cup milk to the peanut butter, and over ½ cup to strawberry."
—Melanie S. from Warsaw, NY

APPLE SLICE NACHOS

Serves 2 to 4 | Ready in 10 minutes

If you're looking for a fun and easy dessert that everyone in your family will enjoy, give this one a try. All of the children who tasted this during the recipe-testing process gave it a 10/10!

Ingredients:

2 crisp apples, cored and sliced

½ cup vegan chocolate chips

3 tablespoons smooth peanut butter

2 tablespoons chopped peanuts

Optional additions and swaps:

Swap the peanut butter for your favorite smooth nut butter

Swap the chopped peanuts for your favorite nuts

Add 2 tablespoons raisins or dried cranberries in step 5

Add vegan mini marshmallows in step 5

Add crumbled graham crackers in step 5

Add unsweetened shredded coconut in step 5

Directions:

1. Spread out the apple slices on a serving plate.
2. In a medium microwave-safe bowl, microwave the chocolate chips for 45 seconds. Mix with a fork until smooth. (If the chocolate is still lumpy, microwave in 20-second increments, mixing in between, until completely smooth.)
3. In a small microwave-safe bowl, microwave the peanut butter for 30 seconds. Mix with a fork until smooth. (If the peanut butter is still lumpy, microwave in 20-second increments, mixing in between, until completely smooth.)
4. Using a spoon, drizzle the melted chocolate and melted peanut butter over the apples.
5. Sprinkle on the crushed peanuts.

TONI'S TIPS:

>>If you don't have a microwave, you can melt your chocolate chips and warm your peanut butter using this old-fashioned but effective method: Place a small pot of water over medium-low heat with a metal or heat-safe glass bowl resting on top of it (make sure the bottom of the bowl doesn't touch the water). Put the chocolate chips and peanut butter in the bowl and stir frequently until completely melted. Monitor closely to avoid burning.

TESTERS' TIP:

>>"You can save time (and a bowl!) by microwaving the chocolate and peanut butter together."
—Claire S. from Salem, MA

MY TIPS:

CHOCOLATE CHIP BANANA BARS

Makes 12 to 18 bars | **Ready in 1 hour**

Extra-ripe bananas aren't just for smoothies and banana bread. The next time you find yourself with some bananas that are a little past their prime, transform them into chocolate-studded bars that are healthy enough to eat for breakfast but taste like dessert. No complicated baking techniques or fancy ingredients required, my favorite!

Ingredients:

2 tablespoons flaxseed meal
5 tablespoons warm water
4 large ripe bananas
1¾ cups all-purpose flour
½ cup brown sugar
1½ teaspoons baking powder
1 teaspoon ground cinnamon
½ teaspoon salt
½ cup plant-based milk
¼ cup vegetable oil
1 teaspoon vanilla extract
1 cup vegan chocolate chips or chunks, divided

Optional additions and swaps:

Swap the all-purpose flour for whole wheat flour
Add a dollop of peanut butter in step 3
For more texture, add ¼ cup crushed walnuts in step 4
For a more decadent treat, press another ½ cup vegan chocolate chips on top of the batter before baking

Directions:

1. Preheat the oven to 350 degrees. Lightly grease a 9 × 13-inch casserole dish.
2. In a small bowl, beat together the flaxseed meal and warm water for 1 minute. Set aside for 5 minutes to thicken.
3. Using a fork or potato masher, mash the bananas in a large bowl. Stir in the flour, brown sugar, baking powder, cinnamon, salt, milk, oil, vanilla, and the flaxseed mixture until the batter is well combined.
4. Fold in ¾ cup of the chocolate chips.
5. Pour the batter into the prepared baking pan and sprinkle the remaining ¼ cup chocolate chips on top. Bake for 50 minutes, or until a toothpick inserted in

the center comes out dry. If it needs more time, bake in additional 5-minute increments until the toothpick comes out dry.

6. Cool completely before slicing into bars.

TONI'S TIPS:

>>These bars freeze beautifully. Allow them to cool completely, throw the bars in a freezer bag, and they'll be good for up to 1 month. If you want to freeze them for longer, wrap the bars individually in aluminum foil before placing them in the bag to last for up to 3 months. To thaw, either leave a (wrapped) bar on the counter for 4 hours (or overnight) or microwave for 30 seconds. If it still needs more time, try an additional 30 seconds.

MY TIPS:

CHOCOLATE AND PEANUT BUTTER DIPPED BANANAS

Makes 4 treats | **Ready in 1 hour 45 minutes**

This recipe transforms bananas into a healthy but decadent after-dinner treat! You'll need 4 ice pop sticks or craft sticks to make these frozen banana pops.

Ingredients:

2 ripe bananas, peeled and halved crosswise

2 cups creamy peanut butter

2 cups vegan chocolate chips

Topping options

Drizzle with more melted peanut butter

Top with unsweetened shredded coconut

Top with your favorite chopped nuts

Top with rainbow sprinkles

MY TIPS:

Directions:

1. Line a rimmed baking sheet with a silicone mat or parchment paper. Poke a stick into each banana half and place them on the prepared baking sheet. Freeze for at least 1 hour.
2. In a microwave-safe mug (the narrower, the better), microwave the peanut butter for 30 seconds. Mix with a fork until smooth. (If the peanut butter is still lumpy, microwave in 20-second increments, mixing in between, until completely smooth.)
3. One at a time, dip the frozen bananas in the melted peanut butter, then place them back on the lined baking sheet. If you're having trouble dipping, you can spread the melted peanut butter on the banana with a spoon. Return the baking sheet to the freezer for 15 minutes.
4. In a separate microwave-safe mug (the narrower, the better), microwave the chocolate chips for 45 seconds. Mix with a fork until smooth. (If the chocolate is still lumpy, microwave in 20-second increments, mixing in between, until completely smooth.)
5. Dip the frozen bananas in the melted chocolate, mostly covering the peanut butter. Drizzle or sprinkle the coated bananas with any additional toppings you like before the chocolate hardens.

You can put it back in the freezer for 10 minutes to make the chocolate harden faster. Store in an airtight container in the freezer for up to 2 months.

TESTER'S TIPS:

>>"If you don't have ice pop sticks, you can use takeout chopsticks cut in half."
—Alfonso R. from Takoma Park, MD

>>"For an easier option, make Chocolate Banana Rounds. Cut the bananas into one-inch chunks before freezing. Dip them in chocolate and freeze again until ready to eat."
—Laura G. from Oak Ridge, TN

CHOCOLATE PEANUT BUTTER BARK

Serves 8 to 9 | Ready in 1 hour 10 minutes

Chocolate and peanut butter are an irresistible flavor combination, and when salty pretzel pieces and crunchy nuts enter the equation, you take that dynamic duo to the next level. This bark has a toothsome bite, but for a thinner bark, try spreading it out on a rimmed baking sheet instead of a 9-inch baking pan.

Ingredients:

1 (10-ounce) bag vegan chocolate chips

⅓ cup + 1 tablespoon smooth peanut butter

1 cup pretzels

1 cup peanuts or other nuts

Optional additions and swaps:

Add another 1 tablespoon melted peanut butter in step 4

Swap the nuts for a mix of seeds and dried fruit in step 4

Drizzle on some melted peanut butter in step 4 before placing in the refrigerator

Garnish with a pinch of coarse sea salt in step 4

Directions:

1. Line a 9-inch square baking pan with parchment paper.
2. In a medium microwave-safe bowl, microwave the chocolate chips for 45 seconds. Mix with a fork until smooth. (If the chocolate is still lumpy, microwave in 20-second increments, mixing in between, until completely smooth.)
3. In a small microwave-safe bowl, microwave the peanut butter for 30 seconds. Mix with a fork until smooth. (If the peanut butter is still lumpy, microwave in 20-second increments, mixing in between, until completely smooth.)
4. Stir the melted peanut butter, pretzels, and nuts into the bowl of melted chocolate, then pour it into the prepared baking pan. Place in the refrigerator for 1 hour, or until completely hardened.
5. Use your hands to break the bark. Store in an airtight container in the freezer for up to 2 months.

TONI'S TIPS:

>>Don't have a microwave? No problem! Simply put a pot of water over medium-low heat with a metal or heat-safe glass bowl resting on top of it (make sure the bowl

doesn't touch the water). Put the chocolate chips and peanut butter in the bowl and stir frequently until completely melted. Monitor closely to avoid burning.

TESTERS' TIP:

>>"Save a bowl and microwave the chocolate chips and peanut butter together for 45 seconds." —Claire S. from Salem, MA

MY TIPS:

DEPRESSION-ERA VANILLA CUPCAKES

Makes 12 cupcakes | Ready in 45 minutes

As the name suggests, this type of cake dates back to the Great Depression, when many Americans couldn't find or afford typical baking ingredients like eggs and butter and had to get creative with pantry staples. The chocolate version of these cupcakes in my first *Plant-Based on a Budget* cookbook is a super-popular recipe, so in this book, I had to give you the option of a classic vanilla version (and a homemade frosting option, too—see page 234!). These cupcakes are my go-to dessert for celebratory occasions, not just because they taste delightful, but because they're so easy to prepare. I'm all about minimalist baking, so when a simple recipe with easy-to-find ingredients comes along, I hold on to it and never let go.

Ingredients:

1½ cups all-purpose or whole wheat flour
¾ cup granulated sugar
1 teaspoon baking soda
½ teaspoon salt
2 teaspoons vanilla extract
1 teaspoon white or apple cider vinegar
¼ cup + 1 tablespoon vegetable oil
1 cup water

Directions:

1. Preheat the oven to 350 degrees. Line a muffin tin with silicone or paper baking cups.
2. In the bowl of an electric mixer (or in a large bowl using a handheld electric mixer), mix together all the ingredients until smooth.
3. Fill each baking cup three-quarters full with batter.
4. Bake for 25 to 30 minutes, or until a toothpick inserted in the center comes out clean. Let the cupcakes cool completely before frosting.

TESTERS' TIPS:

>>"They were very good with gluten-free flour. They were very moist, not too sweet—almost like a little pillow!" —Dyanne E. from Ontario, CA

MY TIPS:

VANILLA BUTTERCREAM FROSTING

Makes about 4 cups | **Ready in 10 minutes**

This fluffy Vanilla Buttercream Frosting is the best I've ever had! It's on the thick side and works especially well for piping. If you'd like your frosting a little bit smoother, add more plant-based milk a teaspoon at a time until you reach your desired consistency.

Ingredients:

1 cup vegan butter, at room temperature
3½ cups confectioner's sugar
2 tablespoons vanilla plant-based milk
2 teaspoons vanilla extract

Directions:

1. In the bowl of a stand mixer (or in a large bowl using a handheld electric mixer), beat the vegan butter on medium speed for 2 minutes.
2. Slowly add the confectioner's sugar while beating the butter. Add the plant-based milk and vanilla and beat for an additional 3 minutes until light and fluffy.

MY TIPS:

ALFONSO'S ARROZ CON LECHE

Serves 4 to 6 | **Ready in 25 minutes**

This recipe comes from the home and heart of this cookbook's talented and wonderful food photographer, Alfonso. He grew up enjoying this comforting dessert in his native Peru and has kindly shared a veganized version of his mother's recipe with us here.

Ingredients:

1 cup basmati rice or other long-grain white rice
2 cups water
3 whole cloves
1-inch piece orange peel
1 cinnamon stick
2 cups creamy plant-based milk (oat milk works best)
¼ cup granulated sugar
1 teaspoon vanilla extract
Pinch ground cinnamon, for garnish

Optional additions and swaps:

Add ¼ cup raisins in step 2
Swap 1 cup of the milk for sweetened condensed coconut milk
Swap the cinnamon stick for ½ teaspoon ground cinnamon
Swap the whole cloves for ¼ teaspoon ground cloves

Directions:

1. In a medium pot, combine the rice, water, cloves, orange peel, and cinnamon stick. Bring to a boil over medium-high heat, then cover, reduce the heat to low, and simmer until the water has evaporated and the rice is cooked, 18 to 20 minutes.
2. Add the plant-based milk, sugar, and vanilla. Stir well, then remove the cinnamon stick and orange peel.
3. Cook for an additional 3 to 5 minutes, until all the ingredients have melded together and the consistency is very creamy.
4. Serve hot or cold, sprinkled with ground cinnamon on top.

ALFONSO'S TIP:

>>This can be stored in and served right out of the fridge—that is how we always ate ours back home in Peru when we were kids. You can also sprinkle a little more sugar on top as a garnish if you prefer it a little sweeter.

MY TIPS:

MEAL PLAN

When I started PlantBasedonaBudget.com way back when, my focus was on developing a site brimming with low-cost recipes. We were posting seven new recipes every week, and I was satisfied with the quality, quantity, and frequency of recipes we were offering. It wasn't until I started connecting with individual people from my audience, however, that I discovered that simply providing recipes wasn't enough. To truly be of service, I needed to explain exactly how to buy and use ingredients, how to make food stretch over multiple meals, and how to efficiently plan for leftovers. That was a huge part of the inspiration behind the first free meal plan that I created for PlantBasedonaBudget.com.

I decided to set the grocery budget at $25 per person for an entire week so that folks who were receiving SNAP benefits could participate, and I'm not going lie, it took *a lot* of effort. But the work was really rewarding, and it led me to create and co-create eight other meal plans at PlantBasedMealPlan.com that have since helped tens of thousands of people along their plant-based journeys. My meal plan was even highlighted in the documentary *What the Health*.

This is a brief sample of what we offer digitally on PlantBasedMealPlan.com, all based on the recipes from this book. For this book, I've kept the budget to $35 per person per week.

GROCERY SHOPPING LIST

Note: This does not include oil, salt, and pepper. For the Bulk items, I'd encourage you to save money by seeking these out in bulk, but you could also buy a larger container.

Produce:

2 apples
1 small cucumber
1 pint cherry or grape tomatoes
3 red or yellow onions
1 bunch curly parsley
1 lemon
1 red or green bell pepper
1 head garlic
4 Roma tomatoes
1 head iceberg lettuce
2 large russet potatoes
1 small zucchini
2 large bananas
3½ cups frozen blueberries
1 bunch kale

Bulk:

6 tablespoons chopped walnuts (optional)
3¾ cups old-fashioned oats
1 pound pasta
¼ cup raw sunflower seeds
2 teaspoons chia seeds
2 teaspoons ground cumin
1 tablespoon chili powder
2½ teaspoons ground cinnamon
¾ teaspoon seasoned salt

Other:

2 quarts plant-based milk
Maple syrup or agave or brown sugar
1 (2.25-ounce) can sliced black olives (optional)
1 (15-ounce) can garbanzo beans
Balsamic vinegar
4 (15-ounce) cans black beans
2 (14.5-ounce) cans diced tomatoes
1 (15.25-ounce) can corn kernels
10-count corn tortillas
Vegan butter (optional)
1 (7-ounce) package fideo pasta
5 cups vegetable broth
1 (8-ounce) can tomato sauce

DAY ONE

Breakfast: Apple Cinnamon Overnight Oats (page 45)

Lunch: Meal Prep Pasta Salad (page 78)

Dinner: Simple Black Bean Chili (page 68)

DAY TWO

Breakfast: Blueberry Kale Smoothie (page 52)

Lunch: Meal Prep Pasta Salad leftovers

Dinner: Potato Tacos (page 108)

DAY THREE

Breakfast: Apple Cinnamon Overnight Oats (page 45)

Lunch: Potato Tacos leftovers

Dinner: Sopa de Fideo (page 56)

DAY FOUR

Breakfast: Blueberry Kale Smoothie (page 52)

Lunch: Meal Prep Pasta Salad leftovers

Dinner: Simple Black Bean Chili leftovers

DAY FIVE

Breakfast: Chia Blueberry Overnight Oats (page 46)

Lunch: Sopa de Fideo leftovers

Dinner: Potato Tacos leftovers

DAY SIX

Breakfast: Chia Blueberry Overnight Oats (page 46)

Lunch: Sopa de Fideo leftovers

Dinner: Meal Prep Pasta Salad leftovers

DAY SEVEN

Breakfast: Apple Cinnamon Overnight Oats (page 45)

Lunch: Meal Prep Pasta Salad leftovers

Dinner: Simple Black Bean Chili leftovers

ACKNOWLEDGMENTS

Paul, bae, my love, my life partner, I'm so privileged and grateful to have found someone who lifts me up and encourages me to dream big. Thank you for holding my hand on the roller coaster that is life, and for helping me stay stable through all the ups and downs. I love you forever.

Sweet Eddie, thank you for being the nicest doggy and best kitchen companion, and for making me feel like a million bucks, even after a long day.

To my parents, George and Lisa Okamoto, for not only bringing me up with the belief system that I can do anything I put my mind to, but for also modeling that it is actually possible. Thank you for making sure I graduated high school when I didn't want to, for pushing me to go to college and graduate when I was 30, and for your patience and support as I found my path. I'm lucky to have a dad and mom like you two.

Lots of love and devotion from me to my brother and sister, Gabriel Okamoto and Elena Deras, and my nephew, Mateo Rowland. And a huge thank-you to my in-laws, Larry and Jolene Shapiro, for caring for me as your own. I love you guys, along with the rest of the Shapiro and Furman families.

To my team at Plant-Based on a Budget, Deanne Thomsen, Alfonso Revilla, Andrea White, Janaye Stanley, and Tina Goyzueta, thank you for stepping up to the plate to help me out while I took some time to write this book. I'm so grateful for the deep care you provide to people who want to eat more plants, and for the support you all show me on an ongoing basis.

It took a village of extremely dedicated and talented people for this book to come together, and I could never have done it without them. To my food photographer, Alfonso Revilla, who moved to Sacramento from Maryland for two months to work on this project—all while being a brand new homeowner and father-to-be. I'm so proud of how far you've come as an artist, and I'm honored to have you on this project. To Lauren Smith, who took the gorgeous lifestyle photos while very pregnant and was kind enough to let me borrow her house for the shoot—thank you. To Tina Goyzueta for managing a team of over 100 recipe testers—that is no easy feat and it's so appreciated!

To my agents, Anna Petkovich and Celeste Fine, for standing alongside me throughout this whole process. To my publisher, Glenn Yeffeth at BenBella, for believing and investing in me and my ideas. To my editors, Claire Schulz, Karen Wise, and Aurelia d'Andrea, for shaping this book with the perfect balance of finesse and personality. Each of you are masters of words, and I'm really fortunate to have you on my team. To my marketing manager, Heather Butterfield, I could write a whole essay on all the reasons you're the best. Thank you for your enthusiasm, care for my success, and most importantly, for your friendship. To Sarah Avinger and the design team, to Monica Lowry in production, and to everyone else at BenBella who has helped me make this book everything I wanted it to be. I'm a really hands-on author, and I'll always be grateful for how available the whole BenBella team makes themselves to authors like me.

I'd like to give a big token of gratitude to all of the nearly 100 recipe testers and their families who helped provide valuable feedback to improve the dishes in this book: Melissa Amato, Justin Au, Kristen Ayotte, Linda Babin, Tanya Baldwin, Zoltan Balla, Toube Benedetto, Dilnaaz Bharucha, Lucie Bigras, Abigail Boring, Anita Broellochs, Dawn Brown, Candice Cadena, Gianna Cannataro, Haley Case, Debra Coates, Lisa Conklyn, Elizabeth Crumpler, Ashley Cruz, Bridget Davis, Ashley Deemer, Mary Demarest, Diane Doyen, Mary Dunbar, Miranda Eber, Dyanne Elliott, Tiina Ennever, Annemieke Farrow, Andrea Garcia, Jami Gerke, Laura Gideon, Caryn Ginsberg, Tina Goyzueta, Jennifer Love Green, Hazel Harbert, Beverly Harris, Evelyn Hernandez, Dana Holshouser, Jeri Jarvis, Cyndi Johnson, Jen Johnson, Micah Johnson, Patty Kadar, Lain Kahlstrom, Shruti Kansara, Hana Kapsch, Patti Kearney, Sheri Koder, Michelle Langlois, Beatriz and Jimmy Leon, Amber Lewis, Yiran Li, Megan Lindeman, Diane Lingo, Lashanda Lomax, Amber Loyd, Amanda Mann, Kaela Marcus, Valerie Marquez, Kelly McAuley, Kelly McLaughlin, Peggy Myles, Christina Nelson, Lap Nguyen, Lisa Okamoto, Nicole Olach, Brooks Peterson, Jennifer Piccolo, Kathlyn Pierce, Paige Puckett, Erica Quessenberry, Anna Rapinczuk, Carlie and Paislee Rhodes, Taylor Roberts, Michelle Rosier, Jessica Sabbagh, Michelle

Salemi, Elana Segal, Jill Sells, Paul Shapiro, Mackenzie Shireman, Hannah Solomon, Janaye Stanley, Jamie Sussdorf, Melanie Swanson, Shari Tavaras, Andrea Waybright, Heather Webb-Carlin, Lisa Wetstone, and Karen Wigg. The recipes wouldn't be as good without all of you! Thank you so much!

Lastly, dear Plant-Based on a Budget audience, supporting you is how I want to spend the rest of my life. Thank you for virtually sharing your stories with me and allowing me to be part of your journeys. I read every comment, message, email, book review, and so on that you send my way. I see you and you matter to me. I'm so privileged to have a community and support system that props me up and gives me so much love and encouragement—the depth of my gratitude reaches down to my core. Thank you, thank you, thank you!

METRIC CONVERSIONS

Abbreviation Key

tsp = teaspoon
tbsp = tablespoon
dsp = dessert spoon

US standard	UK
1/4 tsp	1/4 tsp (scant)
1/2 tsp	1/2 tsp (scant)
3/4 tsp	1/2 tsp (rounded)
1 tsp	3/4 tsp (slightly rounded)
1 tbsp	2 1/2 tsp
1/4 cup	1/4 cup minus 1 dsp
1/3 cup	1/4 cup plus 1 tsp
1/2 cup	1/3 cup plus 2 dsp
2/3 cup	1/2 cup plus 1 tbsp
3/4 cup	1/2 cup plus 2 tbsp
1 cup	3/4 cup and 2 dsp

INDEX

Page numbers in *italics* are to photographs

Q

R

ABOUT THE AUTHOR

Toni Okamoto is the founder of Plant-Based on a Budget, the popular website and meal plan that shows you how to save dough by eating veggies. She's also the author of the *Plant-Based on a Budget Cookbook*, co-author of *The Friendly Vegan Cookbook*, and co-host of *The Plant-Powered People Podcast*. Okamoto's work has been profiled by NBC News and *Parade* magazine, and she's a regular presence on local and national morning shows, where she teaches viewers how to break their meat habit without breaking their budget. She was also featured in the popular documentary *What the Health*. When she's not cooking up a plant-based storm, she's spending time with her husband and their rescued dog in Sacramento, CA.